It is widely acknowledged that this is the age of the moral panic. Newspaper headlines continually warn of some new danger resulting from moral laxity, and television programmes echo the theme with sensational documentaries. This concise guide presents and compares the various different approaches that have been adopted in studies of moral panics and integrates concepts such as 'risk' which have been developed in related fields. With the increasing number of moral panics in recent years triggered by incidents such as the Bulger child murder by other children and the spread of AIDS, this book examines their wider significance, particularly in terms of the functioning of the mass media.

In this book, Kenneth Thompson traces the developments in moral panic studies and also reintroduces some of the initial broader relevance of this field by treating moral panics not simply as separate episodes but in relation to systems of representation and regulation, and as symptoms of wider social and cultural tensions.

Kenneth Thompson is Professor of Sociology at the Open University.

KEY IDEAS

SERIES EDITOR: PETER HAMILTON, THE OPEN UNIVERSITY, MILTON KEYNES

Designed to complement the successful *Key Sociologists*, this series covers the main concepts, issues, debates and controversies in sociology and the social sciences. The series aims to provide authoritative essays on central topics of social science, such as community, power, work, sexuality, inequality, benefits and ideology, class, family, etc. Books adopt a strong individual 'line' constituting original essays rather than literary surveys, and form lively and original treatments of their subject matter. The books will be useful to students and teachers of sociology, political science, economics, psychology, philosophy and geography.

The Symbolic Construction Of Community
ANTHONY P. COHEN, DEPARTMENT OF SOCIAL ANTHROPOLOGY, UNIVERSITY OF MANCHESTER

Society
DAVID FRISBY AND DEREK SAYER, DEPARTMENT OF SOCIOLOGY, UNIVERSITY OF MANCHESTER

Sexuality
JEFFREY WEEKS, SOCIAL WORK STUDIES DEPARTMENT , UNIVERSITY OF SOUTHAMPTON

Working
GRAEME SALAMAN, FACULTY OF SOCIAL SCIENCES, THE OPEN UNIVERSITY, MILTON KEYNES

Reliefs And Ideology
KENNETH THOMPSON, FACULTY OF SOCIAL SCIENCES, THE OPEN UNIVERSITY, MILTON KEYNES

Equality
BRYAN TURNER, SCHOOL OF SOCIAL SCIENCES, THE FLINDERS UNIVERSITY OF SOUTH AUSTRALIA

Hegemony
ROBERT BOCOCK, FACULTY OF SOCIAL SCIENCES, THE OPEN UNIVERSITY, MILTON KEYNES

Racism
ROBERT MILES, DEPARTMENT OF SOCIOLOGY, UNIVERSITY OF GLASGOW

Postmodernity
BARRY SMART, ASSOCIATE PROFESSOR OF SOCIOLOGY, UNIVERSITY OF AUCKLAND, NEW ZEALAND

MORAL PANICS

Kenneth Thompson

London and New York

First published 1998
by Routledge
11 New Fetter Lane, London EC4P 4EE

Simultaneously published in the USA and Canada
by Routledge
29 West 35th Street, New York, NY 10001

Reprinted 1999, 2001, 2002

Routledge is an imprint of the Taylor & Francis Group

© 1998 Kenneth Thompson

Typeset in Garamond and Scala Sans by Routledge
Printed and bound in Great Britain by TJ International Ltd, Padstow, Cornwall

British Library Cataloguing in Publication Data
A catalogue record for this book is available from the British Library

Library of Congress Cataloguing in Publication Data
A catalogue record has been requested

ISBN 0–415–11976–6 hbk
ISBN 0–415–11977–4 pbk

CONTENTS

PREFACE

Although the central concern of this book is with one of sociology's key ideas – moral panics – the title might have been lengthened to *Moral Panics and the Media* to indicate an intention to bring together subjects and sets of literature that frequently overlap but where the connections between them have not been fully explored by sociologists. Moral panics have been the preserve of sociologists of collective behaviour and social deviance. Media sociologists, for their part, have tended to regard moral panics as exceptional phenomena and not central to their field. Furthermore, the 'moral' element in moral panics has tended to be glossed over by those sociologists who have adopted the term, with little concern for its place within a wider sociology of morals (including beliefs and ideologies) (see K. Thompson 1986; W. Thompson 1990a) and in relation to changing forms of moral regulation (K. Thompson 1997). Sometimes panics about food (e.g. the BSE scare about infected beef) or health have been confused with panics that relate directly to morals.

In fact, the theoretical status of the concept of moral panics has been surprisingly neglected. Its meaning is taken to be self-evident and it is used not only by sociologists but also by the mass media. As such, it provides a good example of the explanatory problems faced by social science because they concern a 'pre-interpreted' world of lay meanings, thus involving what Anthony Giddens has called a 'double hermeneutic':

> There is a two-way connection between the language of social science and ordinary language. The former cannot ignore the categories used by laymen in the practical organization of social life; but on the other hand, the concepts of social science may also be taken over and applied by laymen as elements of their conduct. Rather than treating the latter as something to be avoided or minimized as far as possible, as inimical to the interests of 'prediction', we should understand it as integral to the subject–subject relation involved in the social sciences.
>
> (Giddens 1977: 12)

In other words, in the context of studying moral panics and the media, we should be prepared to find the media themselves using this and other social science concepts when giving their own accounts of these phenomena. Consequently, analysis cannot simply be a question of the detached sociological observer, with superior knowledge, passing judgement on 'actors' involved in events or in giving their accounts of them. These people, the 'subjects' being investigated, have to be treated as knowledgeable and skilled interpreters of the events and discussions in which they are involved. The task of the sociologist is to attempt to understand those events and the accounts of them – the different meanings and rationales given to them – as well as other 'facts' or objective information about the events. The reason for mentioning these theoretical and methodological issues at the beginning is that the very term 'moral panics' seems to imply a negative judgement, implying naivety on the part of some of those involved and manipulation on the part of others. Even the word 'panic' might well be regarded as an unfortunate choice, since it has the negative connotation that the behaviour has to be dismissed as irrational. Provided care is taken to avoid jumping to conclusions about the motivations (e.g. manipulative) or mental state (e.g. implied 'irrationality') of those involved, the concept of 'moral panic' can be useful in spotlighting a form of behaviour and pattern of events that is increasingly common in our media-saturated (or media-rich) modern society.

The first chapter will discuss the meaning of the concept and how it developed. This will entail showing how it relates to other concepts and theories. We will then consider some typical characteristics of the phenomena designated as moral panics and the processes through which they develop, particularly with regard to the mass media. Subsequent chapters will be devoted to discussing some of the classic studies of moral panics and to analysing moral panics in relation to specific areas of social concern, such as youth, children and the family, and sex on television.

This book aims to do three things: first, to present and compare the various different approaches that have been adopted in studies of moral panics; second, to develop a distinctive approach that integrates the study of moral panics with concepts and theories developed in related fields, such as the concepts of 'risk' and 'discourse' and studies of culture and ideology, and in terms of reactions to changes in the forms of moral regulation; third, to examine the wider significance of the increasing number of moral panics in recent years, particularly in terms of the functioning of the mass media.

As we will see, the field of study of moral panics was initially developed by a British sociologist, Stanley Cohen, partly building on American ideas on labelling, interactionism and deviancy theory, but at a time when these ideas were giving way in British sociology to more radical and Marxist theories. Subsequently, the subject has been reintegrated into American sociology, with a tendency to lose the initial theoretical cutting edge and to reject the earlier radical concern to disclose the processes of social control and ideological conflict involved in moral panics. In recent British sociology, by contrast, there has been a tendency to dispense with the concept on the grounds that it involves subjecting 'representations' to the judgement of 'the real', rather than concentrating on the operations of representational systems in their own right. This book will trace the developments in moral panic studies and also attempt to reintroduce some of the initial broader relevance of this field by treating moral panics not simply as separate episodes but in relation to systems of representation and regulation, and as possible symptoms of wider social and cultural tensions.

I am grateful to a number of friends and colleagues who have discussed some of these issues with me and stimulated my thinking. In particular I would like to thank Stuart Hall and my fellow researchers on our ESRC project on 'Moral Regulation and Television' – Anita Sharma and Robert Bocock. I would also like to pay tribute to the research abilities of my daughter Clare, who gave valuable assistance.

1

'WHY THE PANIC?' – THE TOPICALITY OF THE CONCEPT OF MORAL PANICS

It is widely acknowledged that this is the age of the moral panic. Newspaper headlines continually warn of some new danger resulting from moral laxity, and television programmes echo the theme with sensational documentaries. In one sense moral panics are nothing new. For a century and more there have been panics over crime, and the activities of 'youth' in particular have often been presented as potentially immoral and a threat to the established way of life. First jazz and then rock 'n' roll were said to be leading youth into promiscuity and antisocial behaviour. In the 1950s there was a panic about the effects on young people's morals of spending time in coffee bars. The 'sexual permissiveness' of the 1960s was believed to be having a subversive impact on traditional family values and feminists were accused of being bra-burners who would undermine family life. In the 1970s it was the image of the young black mugger that became the focus of a panic about law and order.

However, it would be misleading to view the contemporary concern with moral panics as simply a continuation of a previous pattern in all respects. There are two reasons for arguing that there has been a significant change. The first is the increasing rapidity in the succession of moral panics; one barely finishes before another takes its place. Almost anything can spark off a panic, so the initial event can range from something as serious as children killing another child (the murder, in 1993, of James Bulger) to an incident of school bullying; at one time there is fear about being wiped out by the AIDS epidemic, then there is outrage about the discovery of pornography on the Internet. But it is not just the rapidity that is different, it is the all-pervasive quality of the panics that distinguishes the present era. Earlier panics tended to be focused on a single group – teenagers who went to coffee bars, drug addicts or young black muggers. Contemporary panics seem to catch many more people in their net. For example, panics about child abuse seem to call into question the very institution of the family and especially physical relations between fathers and their children, perhaps reflecting a general unease about masculinity and the role of the father. Just as an incident of 'home alone' children raises questions about the 'maternal instinct' and the independent woman.

Britain is not alone in having moral panics, they seem to be increasingly frequent in modern societies as we approach the millennium. But it is not only sociologists who have begun to remark on the extent to which Britain seems have become particularly prone to such outbreaks. It was perhaps symptomatic that Britain's oldest newspaper, *The Observer* (founded in 1791), should devote several pages to the subject after the Queen's Speech in October 1996 opening the last session of Parliament before a General Election. Its 'Leader comment' warned:

> Beware moral crusades. It is true that the British are alarmed and frightened by social fragmentation and growing violence. It is also true that the moral compasses by which to steer are increasingly uncertain. That does not mean the answer is a crusade led by party politicians or conservative newspapers – down that route leads a Dutch auction in repression. Worse, the real dynamics of social breakdown are left unaddressed.
>
> (*The Observer*, 27 October 1996)

This suggests a number of points relevant to understanding the phenomenon of moral panics. The first is that they take the form of campaigns (crusades), which are sustained over a period, however short or long. Second, they appeal to people who are alarmed by an apparent fragmentation or breakdown of the social order, which leaves them at risk in some way. Third, that moral guidelines are unclear. Fourth, that politicians and some parts of the media are eager to lead the campaign to have action taken that they claim would suppress the threat. Finally, the commentator judges that the moral campaign leaves the real causes of social breakdown unaddressed.

Other articles in the same issue of the newspaper sought to address the alleged and 'real' causes of social breakdown, and also outlined the long history of moral panics that stretched back as far as the paper's own history. The more recent moral panics mentioned on the adjacent pages included the murder by two 10-year-olds of James Bulger in 1993, the Dunblane school massacre by an alleged sexual pervert and handgun enthusiast, the murder of headmaster Philip Lawrence by a schoolboy wielding a knife, and the collapse of order at the Ridings school in west Yorkshire. Columnist Melanie Phillips, herself something of a moral campaigner, maintained that 'all these have served as emblems of our time, crystallising public anxiety and confusion' (*The Observer*, 27 October 1996). For her, the question was 'how should society tackle the central problem of the adult flight from parenting' (ibid.)? She joined with others in attributing the ills of society to the decline in family values and moral discipline. However, a fellow columnist, Peter Beaumont, tried to put things in a historical context, pointing out that 'The language of moral panic is not new. It is a complaint that has rung out down the ages' (ibid.). But he noted that the particular concepts defining the problem in terms of family, morality and respectability only 'emerged in their full force as the dominant ideology . . . amid the huge social changes of the last century' (ibid.):

> They gave an identity to a newly-emergent middle class which separated it from what it regarded as the 'vices' of a decadent

aristocracy and the seething working class whose population
was exploding. . . . The problem with its moral crusades was
that they were not only about social reform and fear of crime.
Many – showing their religious roots – also displayed a
morbid concern with sex and the threat to the community of
private 'vice'.

(Beaumont, in *The Observer*, 27 October 1996)

The fear of sexual immorality and the threat it posed to the
family as the main bastion of social order (as religion became
more confined to the private sphere, especially the family) was
allied to a fear of youth subcultures:

The moral panic about sex existed in tandem with an equally
powerful fear of the 'hooligan' or 'yob' lurking on every street
corner. According to Geoffrey Pearson's *Hooligan: A History of
Respectable Fears*, yob culture has been a constant theme of
British society. In Teddy-boys, muggers, each generation has
found a common theme of 'moral and physical deterioration',
blamed on the breakdown of traditional bonds within the family.

(Beaumont, in *The Observer*, 27 October 1996)

Beaumont calls this combination 'the baggage that morality
and family values have dragged through two centuries of social
change' (ibid.). It is part of a perspective that looks backwards to
a golden age of moral certainties from which there has been only
moral decline, in which people – especially the young – can no
longer tell the difference between right and wrong. The remedy
prescribed is a return to a basic set of rules, in the style of the Ten
Commandments, which can be taught in families and schools.

Other contemporary commentators have taken a different
view. According to Martin Jacques:

Contrary to the conventional wisdom of the present moral panic,
society is now a more moral place than it was. Those few basic
rules spoke to a narrow range of issues, turned a blind eye to a
host of others and depended on a largely passive, quiescent and
often authoritarian mode of learning. . . . Far from living in less
moral times, we now live in a more demanding moral climate.

> When I was a boy in the fifties, child abuse, the sexual division of labour, violence against women, paedophilia and environmental awareness, to name but a few, were undiscussed and largely unrecognised. Our moral repertoire has expanded enormously.
>
> (Jacques, in the *Guardian*, 9 November 1996)

To Jacques it was not surprising that the media seemed to present one moral debate after another:

> When morality is no longer a question of a few basic rules, authoritatively pronounced on by politicians and church leaders, then society has to argue, debate, negotiate and rene-gotiate. It is messy, painful, noisy, transparent, often intrusive, but it's far more democratic than the old way.
>
> (Jacques, in the *Guardian*, 9 November 1996)

But, it might be asked, is it really democratic? Is there a public sphere in which serious moral debate can take place and all voices gain an equal hearing? Jacques himself points to some of the disjunctures in the moral arena that make the debate so messy and painful for some:

> There are, I think, two different public discourses on morality. One is unofficial, acted out through the TV soaps and women's magazines, and argued about in the home, pub and office; it is contradictory, revelatory, pragmatic and modern. The other, official discourse, emanates from Westminster and is rarely other than regressive – not entirely surprising given the obsolescent nature of politicians' own culture.
>
> (Jacques, in the *Guardian*, 9 November 1996)

We will see in subsequent chapters dealing with particular episodes of moral panic that this dichotomy of two spheres of moral discourse is too simplistic and does not take account of the ways in which the discourses of popular culture, politics and professional agencies are often combined in the spiral that creates a moral panic. However, he does raise a salient point about the differences between the discourses, which warrants further investi-gation, before turning to the question of how they are sometimes articulated together in such a way as to give rise to a moral panic. With regard to his comments about the mass media, we will need to address the question of whether there is a public sphere in which a rational moral debate can take place. It is a question that has been addressed in various ways by social philosophers in the Enlightenment tradition (such as Jürgen Habermas 1989), by theorists of civil society (Cohen and Adato 1992; Keane 1984), and advocates of public service broadcasting (Scannell 1989). It is also raised by theorists who maintain that the mass media are irredeemably part of the entertainment industry, such as those influenced by the Frankfurt School of critical theory (Horkheimer and Adorno 1972), and theorists of postmodernity (Baudrillard 1981; see the discussion in K. Thompson 1997).

In Britain the dominant political discourse from the beginning of the 1980s and into the 1990s articulated together a combination of neo-liberal individualism and a neo-conservative authoritarian nostalgia for a moral golden age – the age of 'Victorian values'. This discourse has flourished in a period of increasing social inequality, particularly a widening chasm between the prospering majority of the population and a sinking 'underclass'. As Jacques says:

> Some 15 per cent of the population increasingly find themselves shut out of society, living on sink estates, deprived of decent schools, condemned to live on the periphery of the labour market, lacking the necessary technological and social skills to be full citizens. Not for almost a century has any group experienced such isolation and exclusion. It is not surprising that sections of this underclass, feeling outside society, decline to observe its rules, behave in anti-social ways and display a predilection for crime. The language of authoritarian nostalgia is designed to demonise and marginalise these groups and discipline the rest of us.
>
> (Jacques, in the *Guardian*, 9 November 1996)

It seems that politicians on the left as well as the right of the political spectrum have been prepared to play on the fears of the majority, who, despite their relative prosperity, feel anxious about the risks that seem to threaten them. Whilst professional groups with an interest in making claims for more resources, ranging from social workers and teachers to the police and probation officers, are often prepared to provide evidence of a crisis, sections of the mass media, subjected to market pressures, have responded by presenting dramatic narratives with a strong moral content. The result has been an almost bewildering succession of moral panics. It will be argued that the 'at-risk' character of modern society is magnified and takes the form of moral panics in Britain due to the undermining of the authority of traditional elites and the loss of deference on the part of the lower classes, allied to the centralized and 'incestuous' character of the mass media.

THE HISTORY AND MEANING OF THE CONCEPT

The first published reference to a 'moral panic' was by the British sociologist Jock Young, in 1971, when discussing public concern about statistics showing an apparently alarming increase in drug abuse. He observed that 'the moral panic over drug-taking results in the setting-up of drug squads' by police departments, which produces an increase in drug-related arrests (Young 1971). The interesting point about this statement is that it highlights the spiral effect produced by the interaction of the media, public opinion, interest groups and the authorities, which gives rise to the phenomenon which has become known as a moral panic. However, the credit for systematically introducing the concept should go to Young's colleague Stanley Cohen, who used it to characterize the reactions of the media, the public and agents of social control to the youth disturbances – the seaside fights between Mods and Rockers – in 1960s Britain:

> Societies appear to be subject, every now and then, to periods of moral panic. A condition, episode, person or group of persons emerges to become defined as a threat to societal values and interests; its nature is presented in a stylized and stereotypical fashion by the mass media; the moral barricades are manned by editors, bishops, politicians and other right-

thinking people; socially accredited experts pronounce their diagnoses and solutions; ways of coping are evolved or (more often) resorted to; the condition then disappears, submerges or deteriorates and becomes more visible. Sometimes the subject of the panic is quite novel and at other times it is something which has been in existence long enough, but suddenly appears in the limelight. Sometimes the panic passes over and is forgotten, except in folklore and collective memory; at other times it has more serious and long-lasting repercussions and might produce such changes as those in legal and social policy or even in the way society conceives itself.

(S. Cohen 1972: 9)

They key elements or stages in a moral panic according to this definition are:

1 Something or someone is defined as a threat to values or interests.
2 This threat is depicted in an easily recognizable form by the media.
3 There is a rapid build-up of public concern.
4 There is a response from authorities or opinion-makers.
5 The panic recedes or results in social changes.

Implicit in the use of the two words 'moral panic' is the suggestion that the threat is to something held sacred by or fundamental to the society. The reason for calling it a *moral* panic is precisely to indicate that the perceived threat is not to something mundane – such as economic output or educational standards – but a threat to the social order itself or an idealized ('ideological') conception of some part of it. The threat and its perpetrators are regarded as evil 'folk devils' (S. Cohen 1972), and excite strong feelings of righteousness. Events are more likely to be perceived as fundamental threats and to give rise to moral panics if the society, or some important part of it, is in crisis or experiencing disturbing changes giving rise to stress. The response to such threats is likely to be a demand for greater social regulation or control and a demand for a return to 'traditional' values. Much of the literature on moral panics is concerned with trying to explain the motives of those who call for or impose social regulation in such cases – the mass media, pressure groups, politicians, sections of the public, the police and judiciary. However, we should be wary about placing too much emphasis on psychological factors such as stress, or positing motives such as a cynical desire to manipulate or control others. The capacity to tolerate stress varies enormously between individuals and societies, and moral panics can occur in situations where there does not appear to be any discernible increase in stress levels. Similarly, it would be wrong to assume that the motive of actors involved in generating a moral panic, such as journalists and other interested parties, is that of cynical manipulation for ulterior ends; they may genuinely believe what they say. (Although there might be a happy coincidence of principle and interest.) The first task in investigating cases of apparent moral panic is to try to understand the perceptions of those involved, without passing judgement on their beliefs or motives. The next step is to seek to explain why and how a moral panic developed.

Different theorists may emphasize different characteristics of moral panics. On the whole there is agreement about at least two of the characteristics: that there should be a high level of *concern* over the behaviour of a certain group or category of people and that there is an increased level of *hostility* toward the group or category regarded as a threat. However, the use of the term panic means that other characteristic features may be emphasized, such as *volatility* and *disproportionality*. 'Volatility' means that moral panics are likely to appear suddenly and be short-lived; they are similar to crazes, scares and other such forms of collective behaviour. The level of feverish concern characteristic of the moral panic phase is not likely to last, even if the problem itself is of long standing. 'Disproportionality' refers to an implicit assumption on the part of some who use the term 'moral panic' that the threat or danger is more substantial than is warranted by a realistic appraisal (Goode and Ben-Yehuda 1994: 36; Davis and Stasz 1990: 129).

It is the criterion of disproportionality believed to be implicit in the term 'panic' that is most contentious. Criticism comes from two sides. Some critics argue that the term is ideologically loaded or value-laden, so that to dub something a moral panic is to insinuate that the concern is irrational or not genuine. This was the substance of the backlash of criticism against Stuart Hall and his colleagues, when critics contested what they took to be their main argument – that the moral panic about mugging in early 1970s Britain was manufactured by the ruling elite to divert attention from the crisis in British capitalism (Stuart Hall *et al.* 1978). Waddington claimed, contrary to Stuart Hall *et al.*, that the statistics really did reflect an increase in street crime (Waddington 1986; see below, Chapter 4, for further discussion). Consequently, he concluded, the moral panic 'is a polemical rather than an analytic concept' (ibid.: 258) as it lacked any criteria of proportionality to determine whether concern about any problem was justified or not (ibid.: 247). Defenders of the concept have responded that, although with some conditions it might not be possible to determine the extent of the threat, as in the case of future-oriented threats such as the greenhouse effect or the risk of nuclear warfare, there are many other conditions where the degree of risk is more calculable. It is not difficult to think of indicators of disproportionality, such as exaggeration of statistics, fabrication of statistics, singling out a social problem as exceptionally threatening when it is no greater than others, suggesting that conditions at one point in time pose a severe threat when they are no worse than at other times (Goode and Ben Yehuda 1994: 43–5). However, such relatively clear-cut indicators of disproportionality are not always available in situations described as moral panics. Some judgements rest on more 'subjective' factors, as, for example, in the case of differing views about the threat posed by pornography. Whilst it might be appropriate to designate something as a moral panic where it could be shown that fears were exaggerated about the extent of the damage caused to women and children by pornography, some feminist campaigners would still wish to argue that its very existence is an offence to women and, as such, immoral (Goode and Ben Yehuda

1994; Zurcher and Kirkpatrick 1976). In the latter case it would probably be inappropriate to categorize this as a moral panic.

On the whole, most sociologists and lay commentators have a fairly clear sense about what constitutes a moral panic. There are disagreements and difficulties over most social science concepts, but this is one that has been widely accepted and put to good use. Looking back on the same disturbing events that Stanley Cohen first designated as a moral panic, the *Guardian* in 1994 could use the term as a matter of course:

> That nagging postwar British fear of the young, the stuff of Pinky and *Brighton Rock*, Bogarde and *The Blue Lamp*, forties spivs and early-fifties cosh boys, was raised to the level of moral panic via the Craig–Bentley killing and the persistently perceived threat of Teddy Boys.
>
> (The *Guardian*, 12 April 1994)

In 1993 *The Economist* described the publicity surrounding the murder of 2-year-old James Bulger by two 10-year-old boys as another case of 'moral panic'. In both cases public anxiety was amplified by publicity in the press, which portrayed these events as signifying a widespread and deeper moral malaise and as signs of social disintegration.

Britain is certainly not unique in this respect, although it does seem to have been particularly susceptible to repeated outbreaks of moral panics since the 1960s. All advanced industrial societies manifest periodic outbreaks, which suggests that it is a characteristic feature of this social epoch, which has been described variously as modernity, late modernity or postmodernity (cf. K. Thompson 1992). The rapidity of social change and growing social pluralism create increasing potential for value conflicts and lifestyle clashes between diverse social groups, which turn to moral enterprise to defend or assert their values against those of other groups. They do this within a public arena which offers many media outlets for amplifying their fears and articulating demands for social control and regulation to defend those values. There are also increasing numbers of interest groups, or 'claims-makers', with a vested interest in supporting such demands.

Public concern about an issue in complex modern societies seldom develops as a straightforward upsurge of indignation from the grass roots – there is a 'politics of social problems' or, to put it another way, they are 'socially constructed'. Sociologists have distinguished between 'objectivist' and 'constructionist' views of social problems. The objectivist view accepts that a particular phenomenon exists and constitutes a problem by virtue of causing harm or disturbance to a significant section of society. The role of the social scientist is to quantify that problem, to investigate its causes and to suggest solutions. By contrast, the constructionist view is more interested in why and how the conditions or event come to be viewed as a problem. There are various versions of the constructionist view, ranging from the 'strict' to the 'contextual'. The strict constructionist is not very interested in assessing the truth or accuracy of beliefs about a problem, but prefers to study how people 'define, lodge and press claims; how they publicise their concerns, redefine the issue in question in the face of political obstacles, indifference or opposition; how they enter into alliance with other claims-makers' (Kitsuse and Schneider 1989: i–iv). The contextual constructionist takes a more modest position and seeks first to examine the plausibility and factual basis of the claims made in order to support the reality of a problem, but has the same concern about the processes by which the problem is constructed, brought into the arena of public debate and used to shape policy (Jenkins 1992: 2–3). In principle the position occupied by this book approximates to the 'contextual constructionist', but in practice we will be more concerned with the processes of construction of specific moral panics, particularly in the discursive construction by the media and moral campaigners.

The sociologist of deviance, Howard Becker, emphasizes the role of what he calls 'moral entrepreneurs' in defining behaviour and individuals as deviant and criminal. The public is often stirred up through the mass media by the efforts of 'moral entrepreneurs' or moral crusaders, who attempt to rouse public opinion through the media and by leading social movements and organizations to bring pressure on the authorities to exercise social control and moral regulation. Becker describes the moral crusader as fervent and righteous and holding to an absolute ethic; what he or she sees is truly and totally evil with no qualification (Becker 1963: 147–8).

One explanation for the success of such moral crusades in modern society is that they act as symbolic issues, standing in for social discontents of particular social classes or groups. Joseph Gusfield, in his study *Symbolic Crusade* (1963), sought to explain the temperance movement that arose in nineteenth-century America and resulted in national alcohol Prohibition in 1919 in these terms, using Max Weber's concept of 'status defence'. According to this view, formerly prominent ethnic and social groups that felt threatened by immigration and other social changes supported temperance as a symbolic issue that would allow them to reassert their power and their values through legislation:

> Status issues function as vehicles through which a non-economic group has deference conferred upon it or degradation imposed upon it. Victory in issues of status is the symbolic conferral of respect upon the norms of the victor and disrespect upon the norms of the vanquished.
>
> (Gusfield 1963: 174)

This is a view that has subsequently been adopted in studies of pressure groups against drugs, abortion and pornography (e.g. Zurcher and Kirkpatrick 1976). However, Roy Wallis, in his study of the National Viewers' and Listeners' Association (NVALA) – founded in Britain in 1964 by Mary Whitehouse to stem a perceived threat to moral standards from television – concluded that there was no reason to doubt the participants' own explanation, that it was the increasing disparity between the moral standards they had been brought up with and those in contemporary society that provided the grounds for commitment to this moral reform movement (Wallis 1976). We will return to this example in a later chapter, but it illustrates the point that a single-factor explanation, such as loss of status, may be too simple to explain the rise and persistence of a moral reform movement, let alone something as effervescent as a moral panic episode. Although moral panic episodes may recur at intervals, it is worth bearing in mind their collective-behaviour-like quality, which Cohen referred to in his original discussion of the phenomenon. According to Goode, collective behaviour is defined as behaviour that is relatively spontaneous, volatile, evanescent, emergent, extra-institutional, and short-lived; it emerges in situations in which there is a lack of clear-cut definitions as to what to do from mainstream culture:

> Collective behaviour operates outside the stable, patterned structures of society; it reflects the 'maverick' side of human nature. Compared with conventional, everyday life, collective behaviour is less inhibited and more spontaneous, more changeable and less structured, short-lived and less stable.
>
> (Goode and Ben-Yehuda 1994: 104)

As Goode and Ben-Yehuda point out, S. Cohen's original (1972) description refers to a number of forms of collective behaviour that have direct relevance to moral panics: mass hysteria (p. 11), mass delusion (pp. 11, 148), disasters (pp. 11, 144ff.), including the convergence process during disasters (p. 159), riots (p. 11), including race riots (p. 155), crowds (p. 11), especially the milling process that takes place during crowd assemblies (p. 154), mass vilification (pp. 11–12), rumours (pp. 155–6) and legends (p. 156).

It is this similarity to other forms of collective behaviour and its episodic characteristic that, according some American sociologists, distinguishes the moral panic from other types of action associated with social problems, such as the activities of pressure groups, social movements or grassroots protest movements of people directly threatened by the behaviour in question. This distinction is important in trying to understand why some sociologists have concluded that contemporary Britain has been particularly susceptible to episodes that are widely characterized as moral panics:

> Moral panic theory has been extremely influential in Great Britain. It has been applied more recently to concern over 'baby-battering' or child physical abuse (Parton 1979, 1981,

1985a), to AIDS (Vass 1986; Porter 1986), to British 'dole scroungers' or welfare cheats (Golding and Middleton 1982), and to the domestic heroin 'crisis' of the early 1980s (Pearson *et al.* 1987). Pornography campaigns and censorship have been fruitful sources of material in this area, notably for the attempt in the early 1980s to close sex shops and to ban violent 'video nasties' (Barker 1984; Taylor 1987; [W.] Thompson 1989, 1990b).

(Jenkins 1992: 7)

Jenkins stresses a combination of contextual factors, such as political and socio-economic trends (Thatcherism, unemployment, an increase in the number of working mothers, decline of the nuclear family, immigration and loss of sovereignty to Europe problematizing national identity, feminism and gay politics) and the existence of exceptionally large readership of a national tabloid press, to account for the fact that there has been this proliferation of moral panics in Britain. Another important intermediate factor between changes in the social context and the amplification of threats by the mass media is that of interest groups. If the social changes provided the grounds for anxiety and the media gave those fears publicity, in each panic Jenkins found a number of influential claims-makers, each with a set of interests or a political agenda. It seemed that a crucial role was played by various types of moral entrepreneurs and interest groups: 'individuals, pressure groups, and bureaucratic agencies, each with a complex and often shifting pattern of alliances between them' (Jenkins 1992: 10). Consequently, the examples discussed by Jenkins tend to support an *interest group theory* of moral panics and moral crusades, though he acknowledges there was also some evidence for the alternative theory, such as in Cohen's account of the Mods and Rockers panic, in terms of a *politics of anxiety theory*, according to which panics served to reassert the dominance of an established value system at a time of perceived anxiety and crisis, and folk devils provided a necessary external threat (S. Cohen 1972; Pearson 1983). Whereas Stuart Hall *et al.* (1978), in their analysis of the scare about muggings in the early 1970s, are described as adopting a Marxist perspective that was closer to an interest theory, suggesting that it was no coincidence that the muggings panic arose at a time of severe economic crisis and unemployment, so that increased social fears helped to justify police actions against the 'reserve army of the unemployed', against the young, poor, and black; while barely concealed racist rhetoric served to divert the working class from united action (Jenkins 1992: 7).

In our discussion of various case studies we will draw on a range of theories, but the main emphasis will be on the role of the mass media in relation to cultural politics and the politics of anxiety in the 'risk society'. It is this aspect that has been least developed in the literature on moral panics, and it is also the factor that seems most likely to explain the frequency and spread of moral panics in Britain. American sociologists have tended to emphasize social psychological factors, such as anxiety and stress, portraying moral panics as just another form of collective behaviour, or in terms of interest groups and social movements; whilst, for a period beginning in the mid-1970s, British studies such as Stuart Hall *et al.* portrayed moral panics mainly in terms of a crisis of capitalism and a consequent increase in state authoritarianism. However, it can be argued that some of the most useful contributions of each of these approaches have yet to be fully combined into an explanatory framework. The American studies have been particularly insightful in their analyses of the role of moral entrepreneurs and claims-makers. But the influence of these opinion leaders depends on publicity through the mass media. And it could be argued that the originality of the work of Hall and his colleagues at the Birmingham Centre for Contemporary Cultural Studies lay not so much in their use of Marxist concepts and theories concerning capitalism and the state, but rather in their pioneering and imaginative approach to cultural studies as symbolic politics, particularly their analyses of subcultures and the 'signification spiral' – a way of publicly signifying issues and problems which is intrinsically escalating, i.e. 'it increases the perceived potential threat of an issue through the way it becomes signified' (Stuart Hall and Jefferson 1976: 77).

Although sociologists aspire to develop a universalistic science and to avoid theoretical ethnocentrism, there can be no doubt that different national conditions lead to differences of theoretical emphasis. Whilst it is true that American sociologists took up the concept of moral panics with some enthusiasm after it originated in Britain, there are clear differences of emphasis. For example, Goode and Ben-Yehuda incorporate the concept into the fields of social movements and collective behaviour studies, which have a prominent place in American sociology, whereas Cohen made only passing references to social movements and collective behaviour (S. Cohen 1972: 120). Social movements are defined as organized efforts by a substantial number of people to change or resist change in some important aspect of society, and their principal aim is to establish the legitimacy of a specific claim about a social condition (Goode and Ben-Yehuda 1994: 116). Social movements are distinguished from *established pressure groups* or *lobbies*, on the grounds that they are mainly composed of outsiders without direct access to policy-makers and legislators, and their statements do not receive automatic attention in the media. In order to further their claims they have to gain the media's attention and attempt to secure legitimation for their definition of the reality of the condition being addressed. They do this by painting their issue in terms of good versus evil, and the language of moral indignation. The focus is on the worst aspects of the condition they are denouncing as if these are typical and representative. For example, a moral panic about pornography may be generated by focusing exclusively on pornography involving children or violence, even though these constitute a small proportion of pornography (Goode and Ben-Yehuda 1994: 120).

Goode and Ben-Yehuda distinguish between a *'middle level' outsider interest groups (or social movements) model* of moral panics, a *grassroots model* and an *elite-engineered model*. On the whole, they themselves favour the 'middle level' approach, although they accept that some attention should be paid to the other two levels.

The grassroots model sees moral panics as a direct and spontaneous expression of a widespread concern and anxiety about a perceived evil threat. An often cited example was the outbreak of fear over the threat of witches which led to the Salem witchcraft trials in seventeenth-century Massachusetts (Erikson 1966). There was no interest group or elite that stood to gain from engineering such fears, although the general effect of coming together to punish the deviant offenders was to produce a greater sense of social and moral solidarity at a time of change and uncertainty (Erikson takes it to be an example of a strengthening of what Emile Durkheim (1933) called the 'collective conscience').

Proponents of an elite-engineered model are said to be critical of such a grassroots model explanation, arguing that crime and the repression of crime are important in 'enabling the ruling stratum to maintain its privileged position' (Chambliss and Mankoff 1976: 15–16). However, Goode and Ben-Yehuda tend to confuse an 'elite model' with a 'class model'. The former refers to a social group whose main concern is to maintain their privileged social status, whereas a class model is concerned with the reproduction of a structure of socio-economic relations (i.e. capitalist social relations). In the latter model the tendency has been to look at the ways in which the state, through institutions such as the media, social workers, the police and the courts, maintains and reproduces the social order. The portrayal of the muggings panic in 1970s Britain by Stuart Hall *et al.* is cited by Goode and Ben-Yehuda as an illustration of an elite-engineered theory of moral panics. This is because it specifically focused on questions such as 'What forces stand to benefit from it? What role has the state played in its construction? What real fears is it mobilising?' (Stuart Hall *et al.* 1978: viii). However, Stuart Hall *et al.* insisted that they were not presenting a 'conspiratorial' interpretation in which an elite consciously plotted to maintain their power and privileges. It is true that at times their language did seem to be arguing that the ruling elite orchestrates hegemony, and as a result manages to convince the rest of society – the press, the general public, the courts, law enforcement – that the real enemy is not the crisis in British capitalism but the criminal and the lax way he has been dealt with. However, this suggestion of a conscious strategy on the part of a group of people, the 'elite', is not typical of their analysis. On the whole their emphasis is on structural tendencies, the ways in which institutions tend to favour certain interpretations of events that have the effect of maintaining social order, because they are 'structured in dominance'. In other words, the media tend to 'reproduce the definitions of the powerful' (Stuart Hall *et al.* 1978: 57); they 'faithfully and impartially . . . reproduce symbolically the existing structure of power in society's institutional order' (ibid.: 58). The media, especially, do not necessarily consciously set out to generate a moral panic with the intention of diverting attention from economic problems, but economic problems create strains and the media respond by amplifying the symptoms of strain, such as fears about a breakdown in law and order.

American sociologists have been less inclined than their British counterparts to look for society-wide cultural and social structural explanations such as crises of capitalism and cultural hegemony (although there are exceptions, as in the case of Chambliss and Mankoff 1976). Goode and Ben-Yehuda are more typical in preferring an interest-group theory of moral panics, arguing that moral panics are more likely to emanate from the middle rungs of the power and status hierarchy. In the interest-group perspective, 'professional associations, police departments, the media, religious groups, educational organizations, may have an independent stake in bringing an issue to the fore – focusing media attention on it or transforming the slant of news stories covering it, alerting legislators, demanding stricter law enforcement, instituting new educational curricula, and so on' (Goode and Ben-Yehuda 1994: 139). And it is true that these middle-range theories are extremely serviceable for explaining the immediate causes of individual moral panics, particularly the role of moral entrepreneurs who launch crusades that may become panics. What they do not explain is the multiplicity or rapid succession of moral panics in a particular period. Furthermore, because they define the media as simply another middle-range interest group they do not explain the convergence or the linking by labelling of the specific issue to other problems, which is an element in the 'signification spiral' discussed by Stuart Hall and Jefferson (1978):

Convergence occurs when two or more activities are linked in the process of signification as to implicitly or explicitly draw parallels between them. Thus the image of 'student hooliganism' links student protest to the separate problem of hooliganism – whose stereotypical characteristics are already part of socially available knowledge.... In both cases, the net effect is amplification, not in the real events being described but in their threat potential for society.

(Stuart Hall *et al.* 1978: 223).

A signification spiral does not exist in a vacuum. It can only work if the connecting links are easily established by drawing on pre-existing ideological complexes or discursive formations. Philip Jenkins, in his study of contemporary British moral panics, whilst insisting that there was insufficient evidence to support the political processes suggested in the 'Marxist' account of Stuart Hall *et al.*, did agree that it provides strong confirmation for viewing panics as interdependent and he regretted that the issue of interdependence was not frequently discussed (Jenkins 1992: 12). However, although Jenkins admits that moral panics tend to appear in groups rather than singly, and that they are related to wider anxieties and social contextual factors, he tends to focus most of his explanation on claims-makers and interest groups. He believes that this is now justified for explaining even British moral panics because Britain has become more like America:

Like many European countries, British society in the last two decades has become more oriented to the politics of interest groups than to traditional notions of class, and issues of race, ethnicity, and gender have become pivotal. British politics in the 1960s and 1970s were dominated by issues with a powerful and overt class content: union power, regulation of strikes and industrial conflict, nationalization of industry. In the 1980s, the emphasis shifted to interest group politics and social issues such as censorship, feminism, gay rights, education, and public morality (which is not to say that a class agenda may not underlie many or most of these issues). In all of these areas, debate would be conditioned by moral panics, by stereotypes of sexual violence and threatening sexual predators.

(Jenkins 1992: 46)

Jenkins is right to point out the growth of interest groups and claims-makers, and their pursuit of '*symbolic politics* and the '*politics of substitution*', through which they drew attention to a specific problem in part because it symbolized another issue, which they could not address directly. For example, the decriminalization of homosexuality meant that those who wished to denounce such practices as immoral had to do this in an indirect way by raising fears about the threat to children and the supposed upsurge of paedophilia. He also refers to some of the fundamental cultural and social changes making for a politics of anxiety underlying the symbolic politics represented in moral panics, such as those over child sexual abuse within the family (1985–7), paedophile sex rings (1987–9), the alleged wave of child murder cases (1986–90) and similar cases. Many of these factors combined to unsettle traditional gender relations and ideas about sexuality, particularly with regard to women's roles, the family and the care of children. The economic changes included a worldwide slump, increased competition between western and eastern capitalist economies, a shift from manufacturing to service industries, an increase in the female workforce (including working mothers), and a decline of economic activity in old industrial and inner city areas. The corresponding political changes included a return to neo-liberal, free-market policies and pressures to cut welfare state benefits that had provided a safety net for the victims of economic change, which in turn increased insecurity for many groups. Many of the moral panics that accompanied these profound social changes could well be interpreted in terms of the politics of anxiety, symbolic politics or the politics of substitution.

Two theoretical streams that have not yet been incorporated into the explanation of moral panics are those emanating from Ulrich Beck's concept of *risk society* (Beck 1992) and Michel Foucault's work on *discursive formations* (Foucault 1971). The concept of risk society is relevant to developing the politics of anxiety explanation of moral panics. Whilst Foucault's work on discursive formations could help in developing the ideas about the signification spiral and the process of convergence, discussed by Hall and his colleagues.

RISK SOCIETY

Beck argues that, whereas in earlier stages of modernization the main problems were concerned with the production of wealth and its distribution, as societies become highly modernized they produce more risks for their members and also become more conscious of these risks:

> The gain in power from techno-economic 'progress' is being increasingly overshadowed by the production of risks. In an early stage, these can be legitimated as 'latent side effects', As they become globalized, and subject to public criticism and scientific investigation, they come, so to speak, out of the closet and achieve a central importance in social and political debates. This 'logic' of risk production and distribution is developed in comparison to the 'logic' of distribution of wealth (which has so far determined social-theoretical thinking). At the centre lie the risks and consequences of modernization, which are revealed as irreversible threats to the life of plants, animals and human beings. Unlike the factory-related or occupational hazards of the nineteenth and the first half of the twentieth centuries, these can no longer be limited to certain localities or groups, but rather exhibit a tendency to globalization which spans production and reproduction as much as national borders, and in this sense brings into being supranational and non-class-specific global hazards with new types of social and political dynamism.
>
> (Beck 1992: 12–13)

There are two points to note here. The first is that modernization increases risks and makes people more rather than less conscious of being at risk. The second point is that sociological theory and analysis should be more concerned with problems of risk and fear of risk than with theories and concepts that derive from an earlier period of modernization when the main problems concerned wealth production and distribution. The suggestion is that we need a sociology of 'risk society' to replace the centrality of concepts such as 'industrial' or 'class society', which were the focus of classical sociology as exemplified by the likes of Marx and Weber. Beck's depiction of the risks and consciousness of risks inherent in advanced modern societies corresponds in some respects to the politics of anxiety account of moral panics.

Similarly, Mary Douglas considers public concern about crime and deviance within a general analysis of responses to risk and argues that one can use public perceptions of risky or frightening subjects as a 'lens for sharpening the focus on the social organization itself' (1986: 92). She adopts a Durkheimian theoretical framework in suggesting that 'the morally punitive cosmos uses risks to uphold community' (ibid.: 97). It follows from this that it is often the case that 'reactive traditionalism' (Giddens 1990: 158) and other varieties of authoritarianism focus upon the felt failure of law enforcement and punishment as morally central institutions as a primary argument for the reassertion of the forces of order (Sparks 1992: 32; see also Garland 1990: 237). The Durkheimian argument that public indignation about social deviance is functionally beneficial for recreating social unity was echoed by Karl Marx in *Theories of Surplus Value* when he states that the criminal 'renders a "service" by arousing the moral and aesthetic feelings of the public' (1968, part 1: 387). Politicians have not been slow to adopt a populist 'law and order' agenda when public opinion has been incited by mass media stories about mounting risks from a range of threats from socially deviant behaviour. The mass media, for their part, are interested in dramatic stories, and studies of public awareness of risks show that dramatic events are judged to be more common than less dramatic events. Thus, although disease takes a hundred times as many lives as homicide in America, newspapers contain three times as many articles on death from homicides as death from disease (Slovic *et al.* 1980). The extent of fear of crime in a community is less strongly correlated with actual crime rates than with the amount of news about crime

– and the treatment or process of manufacture of that news – in the media (Goode and Ben-Yehuda 1994: 97; cf. Fishman 1980, on the manufacture of news).

DISCOURSES AND DISCURSIVE PRACTICES

Some recent contributors to social theory, such as Michel Foucault, have tended to move away from these more 'functionalist' explanations. He argued that modern systems of social control have ceased to depend on public dramas of transgression and retribution, relying instead on a dispersed 'capillary' network of private and institutional 'disciplinary' mechanisms. Foucault's interest in his early works was in the rules and practices that produced statements and regulated discourse in different periods and social domains. By discourse he meant 'a group of statements which provide a language for talking about – a way of representing – the knowledge about a particular topic at a particular historical moment' (Hall 1992: 291). Discourses never consist of one statement, one text or one source. The same discourse, characteristic of the way of thinking or state of knowledge about a topic (what Foucault called the *episteme*) will appear across a range of texts and at a number of different institutional sites within society. When these different statements 'refer to the same object, share the same style and . . . support a strategy . . . a common institutional pattern . . . or political drift or pattern' (Hall 1992: 291), then they are said by Foucault to belong to the same *discursive formation*.

In his later work Foucault paid less attention to the production of knowledge through discourse and became more concerned with how knowledge was put to work in the regulation of the conduct and behaviour of others through what he called *discursive practices* in specific institutional settings. His object of study was the relationship between knowledge and power, which he saw as intimately linked, and how power operated within what he called the *apparatus* and its *technologies*. Power was exercised through the apparatus by means of specific techniques and practices – its 'technologies'. He called his particular form of investigation 'genealogical'. Genealogy took as its focus the relations between knowledge, power and the body in modern society. It saw knowledge as enmeshed in relations of power because it was always being applied to the regulation of social conduct in practice. His approach differed from the classical sociological and Marxist theories of ideology, which sought to identify class interests concealed within particular forms of knowledge. Foucault shifts attention away from questions of truth and repressive power – the hallmarks of theories of ideology – to a focus on how a discursive formation constitutes a regime of truth and how power is not simply a top-down imposition, but circulates productively at all levels. The efforts to control sexuality, for example, produce an explosion of discourses about sex – television and radio programmes, magazine and newspaper articles (and pictures), novels, legislation, medical and counselling advice, research programmes and learned articles, as well as the pornographic industry. Whilst not denying that the state or a ruling class may have positions of dominance, Foucault shifts attention away from top-down strategies of power, towards the many localized circuits, tactics, mechanisms and effects through which power operates – the 'micro-physics' of power. Power circulates at all levels of society in a sort of 'capillary' movement, rather than in unilinear top-down movement. The main object of the micro-physics of power in Foucault's model is the body. The body is at the centre of the struggles between different formations of power/knowledge. It is to the body that the techniques of regulation are applied. Different discursive formations and apparatuses divide, classify and inscribe the body differently in their respective regimes of power and 'truth'. His focus is on historical ruptures and breaks, in the change from one discursive regime to another.

The contribution of Foucault to the understanding of moral panics has yet to be made, but it could lie in viewing controversies over various aspects of sexuality as signs of struggle over rival discourses and regulatory practices. Foucault's key point about the history of regimes of truth concerning sexuality is that we should not be guided by the idea that Victorian society was characterized by a repressive and censoring discourse about sex, in contrast with our own freer situation. Modern society throughout its history should be characterized in terms of a positive drive to know the 'truth' about sex and to create a 'science of sex', even though repression and censorship might have had 'a local and practical role to play in a transformation into discourse, a technology of power, and a will to knowledge' (Foucault 1976/80: 3–11). Foucault's aim was not to overthrow the idea that we had passed from a repressive Victorian morality to a freer and more open contemporary view of sex, but to advocate a more exact plotting of the different links between discourses at various times:

> The doubts I would like to oppose to the repressive hypothesis are aimed less at showing it to be mistaken than at putting it back within a general economy of discourses on sex in modern societies since the seventeenth century. Why has sexuality been so widely discussed, and what has been said about it? What were the effects of power generated by what was said? What are the links between these discourses, these effects of power, and the pleasures that were invested by them? What knowledge (*savoir*) was formed as a result of this linkage? The object, in short, is to define the regime of power–knowledge–pleasure that sustains the discourse on human sexuality in our part of the world.
>
> (Foucault 1976/80: 11)

The relevance of Foucault's comments about discourses of sexuality and power is that it alerts us to the fact that moral panics about sexuality, and other issues, represent power struggles over moral regulation. Contemporary society is characterized by a profusion of discourses about sexuality and the regulation of bodies, each with different moral implications, and these are frequently in conflict. Not surprisingly, therefore, the mass media reflect those conflicts and amplify them, often giving rise to a spiral effect that results in what we have termed a 'moral panic'. This is more likely to be the case where several examples of deviant behaviour can be linked to some more general risk from moral degeneracy, such as a threat to children from child abusers, pornography, video nasties, homosexuality, violence on television, etc.

MASS MEDIA AND THE PUBLIC SPHERE

Britain presents an interesting test case for studying the phenomenon of moral panics in modern society because, since the 1970s, it has experienced such a rapid succession of such episodes sweeping through the whole society. One reason for this is the nature of the mass media in Britain. Britain is exceptional for the extent to which it has national mass media that are highly concentrated and closely linked. Whereas in societies such as America and France the press is mainly regional and local rather than national, in Britain the reverse is the case – the London-based national newspapers are dominant. Even when stories originate in local papers, they are quickly picked up by the national press if they have a broader news value. (This is one of the reasons why we will concentrate mainly on newspaper reports in the case of British moral panics.) Similarly with regard to television, the five terrestrial channels have a national outreach and often echo the news agenda set by the press. Since the 1970s there has been growing competition to increase readership between the still large number of national newspapers and to increase viewing figures for each of the television channels. The pace of competition was accelerated by the acquisition by Rupert Murdoch's News International Corporation of newspapers at both ends of the market – the *Sun*, developing it into the biggest-selling tabloid daily (circulation 4 million in 1995), and the biggest-selling Sunday paper, *News of the World* (4.8 million), complemented by the most prestigious of the daily broadsheets, *The Times*, and the most widely read of the 'serious' Sunday papers, *The Sunday Times*. The *Sun* has been accused of adopting an aggressively down-market style of presentation, including material that in the United States would have been considered only suitable for supermarket tabloids like the *National Enquirer*, which are not regarded as *news*papers. The other major British tabloid, the *Daily Mirror* (circulation 2.5 million in 1995), followed the *Sun* down-market in sensationalism, as did the once relatively restrained middle-market newspapers, such as the *Daily Mail* and the *Daily Express*. In the 1990s the *Daily Mail* took on the mantle of the media leader in the role of moral campaigner, frequently boasting of its successes in influencing politicians to introduce legislation or to take other action to deal with moral issues about which it had campaigned. The broadsheet newspapers were led to follow this moral agenda and to undergo a process of 'tabloidization' in which social problems were personalized and sensationalized. The liberal broadsheets, such as the *Guardian* and the *Independent*, have added tabloid sections, which often contain pick-up on issues raised by the popular tabloids. Even *The Times*, formerly the staid and conservative newspaper of record, felt it had to follow the trend towards sensationalism if it was to compete, and so it gave more coverage to the kind of episodes that have been described as moral panics, whilst adopting a high moral tone to justify its coverage. As Jenkins concludes, 'If the press is part of an "arena" of public opinion in which "the collective definition of social problems occurs"' (quoted in Best 1990: 16), then the size and ground rules of that arena have changed rapidly in modern Britain (Jenkins 1992: 21).

It might be thought that broadcasting in Britain would have remained immune to such influences, in view of the prestige of the BBC and its traditional commitment to a mission to 'educate and inform'. However, the introduction of commercial channels led to comparisons of viewing figures and questions about whether the BBC's charter and its public funding should be continued if it was no longer providing the public with what they wanted. In consequence it was forced to compete with its commercial rivals in providing popular entertainment, including entertaining treatment of news and current affairs. A notable feature of the new programming schedule has been the profusion of talk shows, copied from American television (e.g. Oprah Winfrey), which often take on the kind of confessional character that Michel Foucault found to be typical of modern society (Foucault 1976/80). Documentary programmes, which might be expected to counteract the kind of sensationalist treatment of issues in the tabloid press, have increasingly adopted a format with a personalized story line. One media commentator commented:

It's as if all documentary film-makers now attend Robert McKee's classes on Hollywood narrative structure: He insists on characters to identify with, dilemmas exposing moral character and progressive movement. This fictionalising is limiting and self-defeating. . . . It started as a way of making issues seem more personal. It has become a hunt for ever stranger lives.

(Ros Coward, in the *Guardian*, 11 November 1996)

Coward cited the reception of a documentary programme on adultery, 'Betrayal': 'tabloids savaged the adulterers as responsible for this country's moral decline' (ibid.).

These changes in the mass media go some way towards accounting for the new wave of perceived social problems, and this offered fertile ground for claims-makers – those who wished to make a claim on public opinion and public authorities for attention and resources. These ranged from the swelling ranks of police and social workers to moral entrepreneurs and campaigners. It cannot be said that such developments in the media and claims-makers created moral panics out of nothing. There had to be a social context and constituency that was anxiety-ridden or risk-conscious enough to be receptive to discourses containing a demonizing message. But once such conditions existed, the signification spiral produced by the interaction of claims-makers and the mass media agitating about a social problem could easily produce moral panics.

The topic of moral panics raises broader questions about the possibilities for rational communication and debate in the public sphere. Is it a question of distortions of communication that could be put right by enlightened regulation of the media, as Habermas and others suggest (cf. Habermas 1989; Scannell 1989)? Or are we in a postmodern epoch of media culture in which the public sphere is more like a hall of mirrors where all that exists is media reflections of other media representations, a world of simulations constituting a 'hyperreality' which is immune to rational critique, as Baudrillard (1981) maintains? Other sociologists refer to contemporary culture as overwhelmingly 'a representation through spectacle' or public dramas (Chaney 1993: 33). Perhaps we should think in terms of 'simulated' moral panics, which succeed each other in rapid succession, and are often examples of the media feeding off each other – as in the newspaper-based moral panics about sex on television (discussed in Chapter 8). These are big issues that cannot be settled here, but they do highlight the wider significance of the study of moral panics for a sociological understanding of culture and communication in late modernity or postmodernity (cf. K. Thompson 1992) and cultural regulation (K. Thompson 1997).

In discussing the different moral panics it is easy to become absorbed in the specific issue in each case, losing sight of their wider significance. It is in order to avoid this tendency that we have sought to place the study of moral panics in the context of more general approaches, such as Beck's characterization of modern society as 'risk society' and Foucault's ideas on discursive formations and regulatory practices. The characterization of modern society as risk society alerts us to the ways in which risks increase as changes proliferate, and also to the fact that modern reporting systems increase awareness of risk at the same time that the development of specialist expertise seems to take the definition and control of risk away from ordinary people. The contribution of Foucault's ideas should be to help us to view moral panics as symptoms or signs of struggle over rival discourses and regulatory practices, especially in the cases of moral panics concerning sexuality and the family, which exemplify Foucault's point that it is not simply a matter of progressive deregulation and increasing permissiveness, but rather of new forms of regulation – expert and technical regulatory systems (e.g. counsellors and therapists, medical experts, social workers and regulatory bodies in broadcasting) displacing traditional authorities and their associated values. These broader theoretical ideas are not intended as tools for use in the detailed analysis of moral panics, but they serve to locate the discussions in relation to a more general framework and will be referred to from time to time where relevant.

2

THE CLASSIC MORAL PANIC –
MODS AND ROCKERS

A panic about what was happening to British youth in the 1960s was the occasion for the first sociological analysis of a moral panic (S. Cohen 1972) and this is significant for a number of reasons: first, because concerns about the moral condition of youth have been the object of periodic episodes of moral panic and so they may enable us to pinpoint a major and recurrent source of social anxiety about risk; second, because the moral panic about Mods and Rockers in 1960s Britain provides a good example of the signification spiral by which the interaction of claims-makers, moral entrepreneurs and the mass media results in the establishment of a discourse in which certain groups are demonized as the source of moral decline; third, at least one of the moral panics about youth – that over muggings in the 1970s – has been the subject of the most intense debate between defenders and critics of the concept of moral panic.

The initial episode of deviant behaviour that gave rise to a moral panic and the elevation of a section of British youth to the status of folk devils began in the small seaside town of Clacton in 1964. The rather mundane nature of the event is captured in Cohen's description:

Easter 1964 was worse than usual. It was cold and wet, and in fact Easter Sunday was the coldest for eighty years. The shop-keepers and stall owners were irritated by the lack of business and the young people had their own boredom and irritation fanned by rumours of cafe owners and barmen refusing to serve some of them. A few groups started scuffling on the pavements and throwing stones at each other. The Mods and Rockers factions – a division initially based on clothing and lifestyles, later rigidified, but at that time not fully established – started separating out. Those on bikes and scooters roared up and down, windows were broken, some beach huts were wrecked and one boy fired a starting pistol in the air. The vast number of people crowding into the streets, the noise, everyone's general irritation and the actions of an unprepared and undermanned police force had the effect of making the two days unpleasant, oppressive and sometimes frightening.

(S. Cohen 1972/80: 29)

THE ROLE OF THE MEDIA

Adapting a model of stages of development of certain forms of collective behaviour derived from studies of disaster behaviour, S. Cohen called this the *initial deviation* or *impact* phase. This was followed by the *inventory* stage, in which observers take stock of what they believe has happened. The most important factor was the way in which the situation was initially interpreted and presented by the mass media, 'because it is in this form that most people received their pictures of both deviance and disasters. Reactions take place on the basis of these processed or coded images' (S. Cohen 1972/80: 30). Cohen shows that the media presentation or inventory of the Mods and Rockers events was crucial in determining the later stages of reaction:

On the Monday morning following the initial incidents at Clacton, every national newspaper, with the exception of *The Times* (fifth lead on the main news page), carried a leading report on the subject. The headlines are self-descriptive: 'Day of Terror by Scooter Groups' (*Daily Telegraph*), 'Youngsters Beat Up Town – 97 Leather Jacket Arrests' (*Daily Express*), 'Wild Ones Invade Seaside – 97 Arrests' (*Daily Mirror*). The next lot of incidents received similar coverage on the Tuesday and editorials began to appear, together with reports that the Home Secretary was 'being urged' (it was not usually specified by whom) to hold an inquiry or to take firm action. Feature articles then appeared highlighting interviews with Mods and Rockers. Straight reporting gave way to theories especially about motivation: the mob was described as 'exhilarated', 'drunk with notoriety', 'hell-bent on destruction', etc.

> (S. Cohen 1972/80: 30)

The media inventory of the initial incident was analysed by Cohen under three headings:

- exaggeration and distortion;
- prediction;
- symbolization.

The type of distortion in the inventory lay in exaggerating the seriousness of events in terms of criteria such as the number taking part, the number involved in violence and the amount and effects of any damage or violence. Further distortion took place in the mode and style of presentation characteristic of most crime reporting: the sensational headlines, the melodramatic vocabulary and the deliberate heightening of those elements in the story considered as news. There was frequent use of words and phrases such as 'riot', 'orgy of destruction', 'battle', 'attack', 'siege', 'beat up the town' and 'screaming mob'. Of the total number of arrests (ninety-seven) at Clacton, only one-tenth were charged with offences involving violence, and twenty-four were charged with 'non-hooligan' sorts of offences: stealing a half a pint of petrol, attempting to steal drinks from a vending machine and 'obtaining credit to the amount of 7d by means of fraud other than false pretences' (an ice cream) (S. Cohen 1972/80: 37). The total estimated cost of damage at Clacton was £513. One newspaper reported that 'all the dance halls near the seafront were smashed' (ibid.: 37); but, in fact, the town had only one dance hall and it had some of its windows broken. Similarly, there was use of the generic plural (if a boat was overturned, reports read 'boats were overturned' (ibid.: 39)) and the technique, familiar to war correspondents, of reporting the same incident twice to make it look like two different incidents.

Another element in the inventory was that of constant prediction that the event would be followed by more such events involving even worse consequences, and the assertion this was all part of a pattern due to underlying causes that were gathering pace. Subsequently, similar events to those at Clacton were reported during the following holiday period of Whitsun 1964 at Bournemouth, Brighton and Margate, but all of them were in fact of smaller magnitude than those at Clacton. However, the media coverage suggested that they were getting worse, and it is true that the media publicity had led to heightened expectations of dramatic events, which then attracted spectators eager to witness the drama.

The publicity given to the events entailed a form of symbolization in which key symbols (differences in fashion, lifestyle and entertainment) were stripped of their favourable or neutral connotations until they came to evoke unambiguously unfavourable responses:

> There appear to be three processes in such symbolization: a word (Mod) becomes symbolic of a certain status (delinquent or deviant); objects (hairstyle, clothing) symbolize the word; the objects themselves become symbolic of the status (and the emotions attached to the status).
>
> (S. Cohen 1972/80: 40)

Studies of moral panics associated with the Mods and Rockers and other forms of deviance, as well as research on the mass communication process itself (Halloran et al. 1970), suggest that two interrelated factors determine the presentation of deviance inventories: the first is the institutionalized need to create news and the second is the selective and inferential structure of the news-making process. The mass media operate with certain definitions of what is newsworthy:

> It is not that instruction manuals exist telling newsmen that certain subjects (drugs, sex, violence) will appeal to the public or that certain groups (youth, immigrants) should be continually exposed to scrutiny. Rather, there are built-in factors, ranging from the individual newsman's intuitive hunch about what constitutes a 'good story', through precepts such as 'give the public what it wants' to structured ideological biases, which predispose the media to make a certain event into news.
>
> (S. Cohen 1972/80: 45)

For example, disturbances of various sorts, variously called 'hooliganism', 'rowdyism' or 'gang fights', had been a regular occurrence during the late 1950s and early 1960s in English coastal towns, but it was only with the labelling of the Clacton event as an example of a widespread deviant phenomenon that it became news. 'The Mods and Rockers didn't become news because they were new; they were presented as new to justify their creation as news' (S. Cohen 1972/80: 46). The process of news manufacture is described by Halloran *et al.* by reference to the development of an inferential structure: this is not intentional bias or simple selection by expectation but rather 'a process of simplification and interpretation which structures the meaning given to the story around its original news value' (Halloran *et al.* 1970: 215–16). The conceptual framework used to locate this process, and one which was taken over by Cohen, is that of Boorstin's notion of the event as news. That is to say, the question of 'is it news' becomes as important as 'is it real?' The argument is that:

> events will be selected for news reporting in terms of their fit or consonance with pre-existing images – the news of the event will confirm earlier ideas. The more unclear the news item and the more uncertain or doubtful the newsman is in how to report it, the more likely it is to be reported in a general framework that has already been established.
>
> (Halloran *et al.* 1970: 215–16)

In the light of this, Cohen concludes:

> It is only when the outlines of such general frameworks have been discerned, that one can understand processes such as symbolization, prediction, the reporting of non-events and the whole style of presentation. The predictability of the inventory is crucial. So constant were the images, so stylized was the mode of reporting, so limited was the range of emotions and values played on, that it would have been perfectly simple for anyone who had studied the Mods and Rockers coverage to predict with some accuracy the reports of all later variations on the theme of depraved youth: skinheads, football hooligans, hippies, drug-takers, pop-festivals, the Oz trial.
>
> (S. Cohen 1972/80: 47)

However, although the media coverage may have created an interpretative framework for the events, the media did not operate in a vacuum; there were other actors involved – social control agents such as the police and judges, and moral entrepreneurs, particularly politicians.

SOCIAL CONTROL AGENTS AND MORAL ENTREPRENEURS

One of the effects of the symbolization contained in the media reports of deviance is that it sensitizes people to signs of a threat. Incidents and events that might otherwise not be regarded as connected come to be seen as symptoms of the same threatening form of deviance. After the reports of the first disturbances, all kinds of youth misbehaviour were interpreted in terms of the same symbolic framework. As a result of sensitization, incidents that might have been written off as 'horseplay' or a 'dance hall brawl' were interpreted as being part of the Mods and Rockers phenomenon. Public nervousness increased and there was pressure for more police vigilance and stronger action from the forces of law and order. The police then reacted by stepping up patrols and increasing their interventions in potential trouble spots – seaside towns, dance halls, fairs and other public events. Court proceedings reflected the sensitization. In the northern town of Blackburn, many miles from the seaside resorts where the Mods and Rockers disturbances had taken place, a police officer prosecuting two youths for using threatening behaviour (they had been in a crowd of twenty flicking rubber bands at passersby) said in court:

> This case is an example of the type of behaviour that has been experienced in many parts of the country during the last few weeks and it has been slowly affecting Blackburn. We shall not tolerate this behaviour. The police will do everything within their power to stamp it out.
>
> (*Lancashire Evening Telegraph*, 29 May 1964; quoted in S. Cohen 1972/80: 80)

According to Cohen, the reaction of the control culture was distinguished by three common elements: diffusion, escalation and innovation. Diffusion could be seen in the way in which control agents distant from the original incidents were drawn in, either by regional and national police collaboration, or by defining their own local activities as coping with the same deviant phenomenon. Escalation of measures to deal with the problem was reflected in calls to 'tighten up', 'take strong measures', 'don't let it get out of hand', which were legitimized by invoking the images of those who had to be protected as 'innocent holidaymakers', 'old people', 'mums and dads', 'little children building sand castles' and 'honest tradesmen'. The final aspect of the control culture was that it extended not only in degree but also in kind through the actual or suggested introduction of new methods of control, e.g. new powers for the police and new penalties. Confiscation of bikes was one suggested punishment, and one magistrate went further in suggesting that offenders should be given hammers to smash up their own bikes: 'a childish action should be met with a similar punishment' (quoted in S. Cohen 1972/80: 91).

Perhaps the most important interface in the control culture is that where state control in the form of legislation and legislators meets pressures of public opinion as channelled by claims-makers and moral entrepreneurs. This is particularly important where the moral entrepreneurs are themselves politicians. The initial reaction in the case of Clacton and the other seaside resorts was shaped by local spokespersons, who defined the hooliganism as a threat to local commercial interests. However, they knew that nothing would be done if the problem was defined in purely local terms – the event had to be magnified to national proportions and the responsibility for it shifted upwards. Calls were made for a government inquiry, for the laws to be 'tightened up', for the courts and the police to be given more powers. At some point, in order to have a wider impact, such sporadic general appeals from individuals and local organizations as were reported in the press needed to become formalized into fully fledged action groups. Cohen analysed the process in terms of Neil Smelser's (1963) theory of collective behaviour and the development of social movements. The action groups corresponded to what Smelser calls 'norm-oriented movements', and they developed through a sequence of cumulative stages: strain (deviance); anxiety; an iden-tification of the agents responsible; a generalized belief that control was inadequate; a belief that the trouble could be cured by reorganizing the normative structure itself ('there ought to be a law'); and, finally, the formulation of specific proposals to punish, control or destroy the agent. Cohen also provided a detailed profile of one of the typical moral entrepreneurs, a Mr Blake, who formed an action group, gained publicity for his cause and drew in local politicians and other representatives of authority. This culminated in a resolution in the House of Commons:

> That this House in the light of the deplorable and continual increase in juvenile delinquency and in particular the recent regrettable events in Clacton urges the Secretary of State for Home Department to give urgent and serious consideration to the need for young hooligans to be given such financial and physical punishment as will provide an effective deterrent.
>
> (15 April 1964, House of Commons;
> quoted in S. Cohen 1972/80: 134)

Legislation was rushed through to deal with 'Malicious Damage', justified by explicit reference to the dangers from Mods and Rockers, although the Minister responsible had admitted in the first debate that 'Some of the reports of what happened at Clacton over the Easter weekend were greatly exaggerated' (Mr H. Brook, *Hansard*, 27 April 1964, cols 89–90). Nevertheless, the process had been completed by which a mythology had been created and stereotypes about folk devils had taken hold.

In addition to the control culture, which amplified the deviance, there was also the phenomenon of what Lemert (1952) calls 'deviance exploitation'. Lemert referred to the 'socioeconomic symbiosis between criminal and non-criminal groups' (1952: 310), pointing to the direct or indirect profit derived from crime by persons such as bankers, criminal lawyers, policemen and court officials. There was also *commercial exploitation* of folk devils such as Mods and Rockers by those engaged in marketing teenage consumer goods, who advertised using the groups' style images. The symbiotic relationship between the condemners and the condemned, the 'normal' and the 'deviant' was shown in the media treatment of the Mod–Rocker differences, as in the *Daily Mail* quiz 'Are you a Mod or Rocker?', published immediately after Clacton. There was also *ideological exploitation*, which involves a similar ambivalence in the sense that the exploiter 'gains' from the denunciation of deviance and would 'lose' if the deviance proved to be less real or serious. Such ideological exploitation is not confined to politicians and moral crusaders, but includes a wide variety of groups who could use the symbolic connotations to justify their positions, e.g. 'The men in the BBC who feed violence, lust, aimlessness and cynicism into millions of homes nightly must squarely consider their responsibility' (Resolution passed at the Moral Rearmament Easter Conference, 30 March 1964; quoted in S. Cohen 1972/80: 141).

SOCIAL CONTEXT

The moral panic about Mods and Rockers did not arise in a social vacuum. The media, control agents and moral entrepreneurs required social circumstances conducive to the amplification and willing reception of their message about moral danger. As Cohen explains:

> The Mods and Rockers symbolized something far more impor-
> tant than what they actually did. They touched the delicate and
> ambivalent nerves through which post-war social change in
> Britain was experienced. No one wanted depressions or
> austerity, but messages about 'never having it so good' were
> ambivalent in that some people were having it too good and
> too quickly: 'We've thrown back the curtain for them too soon.'
> Resentment and jealousy were easily directed at the young, if
> only because of their increased spending power and sexual
> freedom. When this was combined with a too-open flouting of
> the work and leisure ethic, with violence and vandalism, and
> the (as yet) uncertain threats associated with drug-taking,
> something more than the image of a peaceful Bank Holiday at
> the sea was being shattered.
>
> (S. Cohen 1972/80: 192)

Cohen suggests that ambiguity and strain was greatest at the beginning of the 1960s. The lines had not yet been clearly drawn and the reaction was part of this drawing of the line. He sees the period as constituting what Erikson (1966), in his study of witchhunts in Puritan Massachusetts, had termed a 'boundary crisis' — a period in which a group's uncertainty about itself was resolved in ritualistic confrontations between the deviant and the community's official agents. Cohen maintains that it is not necessary to make conspiratorial assumptions about deviants being deliberately 'picked out' to clarify normative contours at times of cultural strain and ambiguity to detect in the response to the Mods and Rockers declarations about moral boundaries, about how much diversity can be tolerated. With respect to moral panics, as with the so-called crime waves', they dramatize the issues at stake when boundaries are blurred and provide a forum to articulate the issues more explicitly. The social and physical mobility of the Mods and Rockers — relatively affluent teenagers who could dress in new styles and travel on their bikes outside working-class areas — provoked unease and hostility:

Traditionally the deviant role had been assigned to the lower class urban male, but the Mods and Rockers appeared to be less class tied; here were a group of impostors, reading the lines which everyone knew belonged to some other groups. Even their clothes were out of place; without leather jackets they could hardly be distinguished from bank clerks. The uneasiness felt about actors who are not quite in their places can lead to greater hostility. Something done by an out-group is simply condemned and fitted into the scheme of things, but in-group deviance is embarrassing, it threatens the norms of the group and tends to blur its boundaries with the out-group.

(S. Cohen 1972/80: 195)

This analysis of boundary confusion is particularly relevant in the case of the Mods, whose style and social status did not easily fit established norms. The Mod's appearance was different from the stereotypical hooligan personified by the earlier fashion of the Teddy Boy or the leather-jacketed Rockers, who were thought to be imitating the American motor-bike gangs. The Mods seemed to offer some kind of snub to traditional values through their air of distance and ingratitude for what society had given them. Although there can be no doubt that the Mods' and Rockers' behaviour did seem to pose a threat to the material interests of local traders and property owners in the resorts where disturbances occurred, the sense of moral outrage they evoked cannot be explained in those terms alone. The statements of the moral crusaders who demonized these youth cultures portrayed them as prematurely affluent, aggressive, permissive and challenging the ethics of sobriety and hard work. Psychologists have attempted to explain such responses in terms of the envy and resentment felt by the lower middle classes, supposedly the most frustrated and repressed of groups, who condemn behaviour which they secretly crave. There may be some truth in this, but the fuller sociological explanation that we have suggested needs developing is multifactoral, stressing the interaction of structural conditions, cultural signs and symbols, the actions of key actors and movements, and processes by which typical forms of collective behaviour develop.

SUMMARY OF COHEN'S APPROACH

Cohen's pioneering study of the phenomenon of 'moral panics', using the example of Mods and Rockers, led him to develop a processual model of deviancy amplification, which he summarized in Figure 1.

Initial problem   (stemming from structural and
                                   cultural position of working-class
                                   adolescent)

⇩

Initial solution   (deviant action and style)

⇩

Societal reaction   (involving elements of mis-
                                   perception, e.g. in initial media
                                   presentation or inventory, and
                                   subsequent distortion in terms of
                                   long-term values and interests)

⇩

Operation of control culture,   (sensitization, dramatization,
exploitation and creation of   escalation)
stereotypes

⇩

Increased deviance, polarization

⇩

Confirmation of stereotypes   (theory proved)

Figure 1 Model of deviancy amplification
Source: S. Cohen 1972/80: 199

3

MORAL PANICS ABOUT YOUTH

The subsequent development of the sociological analysis of moral panics in Britain continued to focus, like Cohen's initial study, on youth cultures, and for good reasons. No age group is more associated with risk in the public imagination than that of 'youth'. Of course, imagined risks to children also lie behind many moral panics, especially those concerning the alleged breakdown of the family, but apart from the relatively rare cases of children who commit murder (such as the Bulger murder), children are not usually regarded as a source of risk. Youth may be regarded as both at risk and a source of risk in many moral panics. This is not surprising in view of the transitional status of this age group, occupying a position between childhood and adulthood. It is this very marginality and ambiguity of status that exacerbates the risks associated with youth. Youth presents a problem for social regulation and the reproduction of the social order. But the relationship between the generations and generational cultures is also problematical for young people themselves, and youth cultures and subcultures can be read or decoded as responses and attempted solutions to those strains. In addition to drawing on previous studies of moral panics associated with youth, we will also view these moral panics in the light of Beck's (1992) ideas about an increasing sense of risk in late modernity, and the media representations of these episodes will be subjected to the kind of discourse analysis inspired by Foucault, focusing on moral panics as signs of struggle over rival discourses and regulatory practices.

As we have seen, Cohen's pioneering work on moral panics focused on youth subgroups, such as the Mods and Rockers (S. Cohen 1972), as did much of the subsequent work of the Birmingham Centre for Contemporary Cultural Studies (CCCS) (Stuart Hall and Jefferson 1976). The work of the Birmingham CCCS was particularly useful for theorizing the problems associated with youth, indicating why these might give rise to moral panics, and in developing ways of decoding youth subcultures. In the seminal CCCS collection of essays *Resistance through Rituals: Youth Sub-cultures in Post-war Britain* (Stuart Hall and Jefferson 1976), Graham Murdock and Robin McCron traced the development of sociological thinking about youth and generational consciousness. The most influential early book in the social sciences was Stanley Hall's text *Adolescence* (published in the USA in 1904 and in the UK in 1905). Hall maintained that individual maturation recapitulated the development of the species and that the transition from childhood to maturity corresponded to the leap from barbarism to civilization. Hence, the future of civilization hinged on what happened during the crucial intermediate stage of adolescence. The condition of youth provided a yardstick against which the progress or decay of society could be measured. This idea of youth as a 'barometer' and agent of progress quickly took hold.

The question of how age groups developed a common consciousness was taken up by the German sociologist Karl Mannheim (1952), who maintained that it had its origins in the attitudes and responses developed by particular close-knit 'concrete groups' in the course of responding to their shared social situation. Once crystallized, this generational consciousness could broaden its base and form the core of a new 'generation style' separate from, and opposed to, the dominant style of the adult generation (Mannheim 1952). Mannheim acknowledged the existence of class differences and admitted that 'within each generation there can exist a number of differentiated, antagonistic generation-units' (ibid.: 306). Although published in Germany in 1927, Mannheim's book was not published in English until the 1950s, after he had emigrated to Britain. A more influential book for American sociologists was Frederic Thrasher's *The Gang* (1927), published in the same year as Mannheim's German book. Thrasher initiated the study of youth subcultures, arguing that adolescents in downtown Chicago had responded to the social disorganization of the slum by creating a separate and self-contained social network of gangs with a distinctive culture. When Wall Street crashed two years later it seemed as if the social disorganization had become more widespread, and it was not surprising that sociologists began to see the breakdown of generational relations and the development of autonomous peer group cultures as features not just of slum life but of the general state of society.

With the up-turn in the economy as a result of the war and then postwar reconstruction, America enjoyed a period of economic growth and affluence that gave youth the spare cash to mark them off as a distinctive consumer group with their own tastes and styles. Sociologists, such as Talcott Parsons in an influential article in 1942, 'Age and sex in the social structure of the United States' (Parsons 1942/64), suggested that these developing peer group cultures were localized expresssions of a more broadly based generational consciousness which was crystallizing around a distinctive youth culture centred on hedonistic consumption. This youth culture was seen by Parsons as the culture of a generation who consumed without producing, and whose lengthening confinement in age-specific educational institutions seemed to remove them from the productive system and the class relations that went with it. He argued that youth espouse a different 'order of prestige symbols' located in leisure not work because they cannot compete with adults for occupational status. This American emphasis on generational divisions and the corresponding irrelevance of class divisions, along with the stress on consumption and leisure as the pivots of youth consciousness, came to dominate the sociology of youth for the next couple of decades, not just in America but also in Europe, even though the degree of youth affluence and time spent in education was much less outside America.

There was a sense in which youth were regarded with a mixture of envy and resentment as harbingers of a future in which leisure and consumption replaced the old relations of production at the centre of social life. This could turn into moral disapproval and a fear of social disintegration when the media gave extensive coverage to examples that seemed to suggest 'youth culture' led to behaviour that was 'antisocial', undisciplined and an affront to the values of 'decent people'. Sometimes, as in the examples of moral panics about the youth culture of 'milk bars' in postwar Britain and then rock and roll, the fear was that they represented the spread of American youth culture, which might bring in its train the crime and inner city problems that the British media publicized. Even the man who was to be the director of the Birmingham CCCS when it was founded in 1964, Richard Hoggart, was writing in the 1950s about the 'juke box boys' in terms of a connotative code of threatening 'Americanization', conjuring up a picture of young men 'aged between fifteen and twenty, with drape-suits, picture ties and an American slouch' who spend their evenings listening to 'nickelodeons' in the 'harshly lit milk bars' (Hoggart 1958: 203). The popular magazine *Picture Post*, in an article entitled 'The best and worst of Britain' (18 December 1953), presented a picture of mindless young hooligans 'who revel in attacking old men and women, and hitting people when they are down'; ending with the warning 'We are on the brink of that horrible feature of American life where, in many a shady district, thugs go around from shop to shop demanding the payment of "protection money" or else' (quoted in Hebdige 1988: 56).

The ambiguous image of youth culture as both a symbol of an emerging 'affluent consumer society' and as a threat to moral discipline and order was particularly marked in the media representations of the Mods and Rockers that led to the moral panic of the early 1960s described by Stanley Cohen, as we saw in Chapter

2 (S. Cohen 1972/80). As he puts it, they symbolized something far more important than what they actually did, touching the delicate and ambivalent nerves through which postwar social change in Britain was experienced.

Although Cohen was heavily influenced by the American theories of deviant youth cultures in terms of 'labelling' and 'social construction' (deviance as a product of categorization, a result of the power of some to label others), he also brought to bear some of the British sociologists' preoccupation with structural tensions due to class divisions, not just generational differences. This class element was even more pronounced in the analysis of youth subcultures carried out by the Birmingham CCCS. This was evident in the seminal paper by Phil Cohen, 'Sub-cultural conflict and working class community' (published as the second of the Centre's Working Papers in 1972). Cohen explained the development of subcultures such as the Mods and Skinheads on the basis of the redevelopment of the East End of London, which resulted in the fragmentation and disruption of the working-class family, economy and community-based culture. He suggested that these youth subcultures were symbolic attempts in the sphere of leisure to resolve those problems. The Mods were seen as constructing a stylistic parody of the socially approved but unavailable solution of achieving upward social mobility, whilst the Skinheads were read as an attempt to recover symbolically ('magically', 'imaginarily') the 'machismo' character of the traditional working-class community. By flaunting their 'otherness' in the face of mainstream culture, they resisted being subordinated by that dominant culture and they gained recognition, even if it was in the form of media portrayals of them as dangerous and immoral deviants, so giving rise to moral panics.

As the authors stressed in the 'Introduction' to *Resistance Through Rituals*, Phil Cohen's paper clarified the reasons for their feeling that deviant behaviour had other origins besides public labelling, which led them to relegate labelling and social constructionism 'to a marginal position in favour of a concern with the structural and cultural origins of British youth subcultures' (Stuart Hall and Jefferson 1976: 5). Their subsequent efforts were for some time devoted to filling out Cohen's suggestive framework, initially through papers offering more detailed accounts of particular subcultures – Teds, Mods, Skinheads, etc. These ethnographic accounts are presented in *Resistance Through Rituals*, along with a theoretical overview. However, in 1973, in the middle of developing the work on youth subcultures, members of CCCS became involved in a study of the moral panic over mugging, which had a major impact on their thinking. The sudden appearance of the label 'mugging', attached to a group of crimes which were then said to be increasing at a frightening rate, seemed to warrant a labelling perspective, but the CCCS researchers claimed that this was inadequate and needed to be supplemented by an attempt to relate these activities to shifts in class and power relations, consciousnesss, ideology and a general 'crisis of hegemony'. (We will deal with the mugging moral panic in Chapter 4, but in the meantime it is worth tracing the developments in the analysis of youth subcultures and the consequent moral panics.)

The CCCS explanation of moral panics about youth subcultures is couched in terms of a kind of symbolic guerrilla warfare, in which young members of various class factions symbolically resist subordination to the dominant culture and in so doing provoke a reaction. The mass media share the values of the dominant culture and portray the deviant subcultures as a threat to the moral and social order, and the sensationalized publicity gives rise to moral panics, and an outraged public opinion calls for action against the threat. The main contribution of the CCCS approach was in their imaginative 'reading' or decoding of these subcultures, and in the attempt to interpret these as symbolical resolutions of tensions experienced by their participants as a result of social structural developments. Stanley Cohen, in the 'Introduction' to a new edition of his *Folk Devils and Moral Panics* in 1980, whilst appreciative of these contributions, warned of what he called the 'dangers of romanticism' in this decoding of youth subcultures in terms of symbolic resistance. Taking one example, he criticized Hebdige (1979) and other theorists of Punk who suggest that the wearing of the swastika by Punks (or the singing of lyrics like 'Belsen was a gas') shows how symbols are stripped of their natural context, exploited for empty effect, displayed through mockery, distancing, irony, parody and inversion. Hebdige maintained that the Punks were not generally sympathetic to parties of the extreme right, but Cohen points to other evidence that racism was present among substantial sections of such working-class youth. He is more sympathetic to Hebdige's suggestion that the whole of white working-class youth subcultures – from Teddy Boys to Punks – can be understood as a series of mediated responses to black (American) culture and then the presence of a sizeable black community in Britain (S. Cohen 1980: xxi). And yet, for a long time, blacks (and girls) did not feature as active agents in the subcultures literature, but rather as victims or hangers-on. The mugging moral panic of 1972–3 was a major exception, as we will see, in that blacks were portrayed as likely muggers. And whilst girls tended to be excluded from the violent phenomena associated with the early youth subcultures, Cohen's account of the Mods and Rockers clashes noted that the press sometimes portrayed girls as being behind the disturbances:

> Many opinion statements, for example, drew attention to the role of girls in egging on their boy friends; a letter in the *Evening Standard* (21 May 1964) claimed that the major stimulus for violence came from '... the oversexed, squalid, wishful little concubines who hang about on these occasions, secure in the knowledge that retribution will not fall upon them'. This sort of attribution was supported by inventory interviews of the 'Girls Who Follow the Wild Ones Into Battle' type, although traits other than enjoyment of violence were more consistently attributed to girls; particularly promiscuity and drug-taking.
>
> (S. Cohen 1980: 56)

Angela McRobbie and Jenny Gerber, in their article 'Girls and subcultures' (1976), which occupied a rather solitary position in *Resistance Through Rituals*, commented on the relative neglect of girls in the studies of subcultures. An exception was that of Hippy subculture, about which there were moral panics, particularly regarding its alleged sexual immorality. They noted that girls did feature more in Hippy subculture, perhaps because the middle-class girl students had more freedom to enter into this amorphous culture. Although, in reality, even in the Hippy subculture there seemed to be little shift away from roles which are traditionally female:

> The stereotypical images we associate most with Hippy culture tend to be those of the Earth Mother, baby at breast, or the fragile pre-Raphaelite lady. Again, of course, we must be aware of the dangers of accepting uncritically the images which emerge via press coverage, as part of a moral panic, though the chances are that this panic itself represents the double bind – sexual permissiveness linked with motherhood may be more palatable than aggressive feminism.
>
> (Stuart Hall and Jefferson 1976: 219)

CLUB CULTURES AND RAVES

It is significant that when girls did begin to feature more prominently in accounts of youth subcultures that gave rise to new moral panics, such as in studies of club cultures and Raves in the late 1980s and 1990s, the authors tended to stake out a critical distance from the Birmingham CCCS approach. A typical example is Sarah Thornton's *Club Cultures: Music, Media and Subcultural Capital* (1995), in which the author acknowledges a debt to the CCCS subcultural studies, but then pronounces her study to be 'post-Birmingham' in several ways: it does not regard youthful consumer choices as 'proto-artistic' and/or 'proto-political' acts, where their cultural consumption is ultimately explained in terms of opposition to the parent culture or mainstream culture. In trying to make sense of the values and hierarchies of club cultures, she returns to the Chicago School sociologists of subcultures, particularly Howard Becker on jazz musicians (Becker 1963) and Ned Polsky's work on Greenwich

Village Beatniks (Polsky 1967). In both cases the groups in question drew a distinction between their 'hip' culture and that of the disdained 'squares'. She also draws extensively on the work of the French sociologist Pierre Bourdieu, especially his book *Distinction* (1984), and his idea of groups having different amounts of 'cultural capital' which confer status and power. Subcultural capital is illustrated by the knowledge of 'where it's at' in music and styles possessed by hardcore clubbers and Ravers in the late 1980s, who distinguished themselves and their superiority over the mainstream 'chartpop disco', which they stereotyped as the place where 'Sharon and Tracy dance around their handbags'.

Other studies of club cultures, Raves and the associated drug use (especially Ecstasy – 'E'), have also suggested that the earlier subcultural analysis is no longer appropriate (Redhead 1991; Merchant and MacDonald 1994). Others still maintain that Rave and its predecessor Acid House are nothing new and are merely another link in the subcultural chain, replaying and reworking the 1950s, 1960s and 1970s. Smith (1992) argues that Rave culture is simply a 'third generation' of 'youthful refusals' following in the rebellious traditions of the Hippies and the Punks. Certainly there are some correspondences between this and the earlier subcultures and the associated moral panics. 'As with the Mods and Rockers of the 1960s, the tabloid media, police and moral establishment rapidly sought ways to condemn and control these latter-day folk-devils' (Merchant and MacDonald 1994: 31). The press began raising the alarm about Rave culture in the late 1980s, fastening on to the drug-taking and the fact that thousands of young people were being drawn to the Raves, which were held not only in clubs but also in warehouses, aircraft hangers, open fields and motorway underpasses, often lasting all night. The police were quick to crack down on the supposed threat to public order that the culture posed and new legislation was rushed through in the Entertainments (Increased Penalties) Act 1990. This was followed by further powers, introduced by the Home Secretary in 1993, as part of his crusade against 'juvenile crime', directed against Ravers (and 'New Age travellers' and squatters).

By 1993 illegal Raves had virtually died out, but the Rave/dance culture had spread and diversified into a variety of styles and venues, with no particular class, race or gender characteristics. It continued to attract many thousands of participants and drug-taking was widespread, but press attention had decreased. However, a new moral panic broke out after the Ecstasy-related death of 18-year-old Leah Betts in 1995. A review of the subsequent panic commented:

> Just over a year ago Leah Betts took her first Ecstasy pill. She went into a coma and died. Headline writers had a field day. Sentimental, heart-rending headlines, designed to prey on the worries of ignorant, frightened parents, exploded into living rooms. 'It could be your child', warned the *Daily Mail*. 'Poisoned: Spiked Ecstasy tablet puts birthday girl, 18, into coma', announced the *Daily Mirror*. 'Leah's Last Words: She named Ecstasy pill pusher then pleaded "Help me mum, help me" ', reported *Today*. All the papers used a picture of a helpless, innocent-looking Leah in a hospital bed, tubes sticking out of her nose, an image that would move even the most hard-hearted dance fan.
>
> (The *Guardian*, 16 November 1996)

The article asked the question: 'Why did the Leah Betts affair receive so much publicity?' Other Ecstasy-related deaths (most estimates put the total at around sixty over the previous ten years) had merited only a few paragraphs. The answer suggested was that it was the only Ecstasy-related death where a picture was released of someone who was actually in the process of dying. The Betts parents also undertook a nationwide tour, going into schools and appearing on TV talk shows in an attempt to warn teenagers of the dangers of the drug. Members of Parliament pressed for action to clamp down on night clubs and for councils to shut down clubs if there was evidence of drug-dealing. However, although the authorities and the clubs claimed that they had taken action and the problem was under control, it did not take much to stir up the moral panic again. When the singer Brian Harvey of the pop group East 17 said in a radio interview that 'Ecstasy is harmless' and could bring out the good in people, the *Mirror* (as the former *Daily Mirror* now called itself) gave over its front page to the headline 'ECSTASY SHOCK ISSUE', followed by several inside pages on the subject. The *Mirror* showed him the picture of Leah Betts in a coma and insisted that he recant. It reported that he was close to tears and said: 'It's horrible. She was just a baby. I am so sorry I offended her parents. I did not mean it.' Apparently it was not just the plight of the parents that moved him. He was told that his record company bosses feared a boycott of his records, to which he replied: 'I can't believe they're saying they won't buy our records any more' (*Mirror*, 17 January 1997). His recantation was to no avail; a couple of days later the rest of his group bowed to pressure and sacked him.

Several other papers made this latest E story front page news and it was taken up by radio and television stations. But the *Mirror*, in keeping with its new style of focusing on a single sensational story as part of its effort to compete with its more successful rival the *Sun*, excelled them all in its saturation coverage and 'in-your-face' reporting style. In addition to the full-front-page picture of an Ecstasy tablet, other pages included a full-page colour picture of a Raver with superimposed artist's images of damaged organs; a two-page set of pictures of young people who had died as a result of Ecstasy, accompanied by telephone numbers for readers to vote on questions about what should be done. There was also an account of Ecstasy as a £1 billion-a-year industry, equal to the amount spent on tea and coffee; this was followed, rather bizarrely, by the suggestion that if Ecstasy were legalized it could grow into a £5 billion-a-year business that would yield £4 billion in taxes – 'enough to pay for 10 per cent of the NHS, a quarter of the defence budget, or nearly half the police force' (17 January 1997).

Studies of Rave culture and those engaged in it paint a different picture to that painted by the mass media. They stress the friendly atmosphere, typified by behaviour that is less aggressive, macho and violent than that of conventional night clubs, with more egalitarian gender relations (Evans 1990; Henderson 1992). In assessing the danger from Ecstasy it is argued that it is not so much the chemical substance alone that is the problem but the location of the drug-taking in the conditions of a Rave:

> The symptoms experienced by Ecstasy casualties are similar to those of heat stroke: the high temperatures and vigorous dancing of Raves may interact with MDMA [the basic ingredient of Ecstasy] to produce physical experiences quantitatively or even qualitatively different to when taking the drug in a relaxed state. In America, where the drug has been available for longer than in Britain but where there is no comparable dance culture, there have been only two deaths attributed to the effects of MDMA.
>
> (Merchant and MacDonald 1994: 22)

Clearly there are dangers involved, some of which are difficult to assess, but in view of the fact that millions of young people have been involved in Raves and many have taken Ecstasy, the best policy would seem to be to increase knowledge and education, rather than to sensationalize the issue and risk creating moral panics that young people may react to as scaremongering.

As far as understanding the Rave culture is concerned, the more recent studies have emphasized that it is something distinct from its youth cultural predecessors and needs different theories to those developed by CCCS. Merchant and MacDonald (1994: 32–3) list five ways in which it differs:

1 Rave has been a mass cultural phenomenon among young people, unlike Mod, Rocker, Punk, Skinhead or Teddy Boy subcultures.

2 Rave is not wholly or essentially a working-class phenomenon. Hence, it is impossible to conceptualize it as a symbolic response of working-class youth to material inequalities, in the way that the CCCS subcultural studies did for previous groups.

3   Related to the above, Rave culture cannot be understood as resistance through rituals to the dominant cultural forms in society. In so far as it has offered opposition, it has been directed against attempts to control or outlaw Raves – asserting the 'Right to Party'. Rave culture is essentially hedonistic, concerned with having fun and feeling good, not with changing the status quo.

4   In contrast to the situation prevailing in the subcultures described by CCCS, women are not marginal to Rave culture, it is not dominated by masculine styles of behaviour and it is ethnically mixed.

5   It does not involve all-consuming and easily identified styles of dress in the way associated with Teddy Boys, Mods, Rockers, Punks and Skinheads. Rave culture is not like gang culture; it is more diffuse, disorganized and invisible.

For these reasons, some maintain, it is not appropriate to describe Rave culture as simply another youth subculture. According to Redhead and researchers at Manchester University (Redhead 1990, 1991, 1993), who take a postmodernist perspective and draw upon the writings of Baudrillard, there is little depth to Acid House and Rave and, therefore, analyses which attempt to 'read' and get beneath surface appearances to discover the 'true' (class cultural) significance of youth phenomena are misdirected. The youth culture of Rave is perhaps best seen in market terms, where 'consumers are incited to individualise themselves and where the operations of power seem to favour classification and segregation' (Thornton 1995), but it is hard to regard the desire for classification based on cultural distinction in such circumstances as 'progressive' in the way that earlier theorists viewed dissident cultures as resisting hegemony. However, Thornton also shows that there is still something to be gained in terms of greater understanding by attempting to 'read' or decode the symbolic distinctions contained in the discourses and practices of Rave culture – they can tell us something about how different groups seek to distinguish themselves from the perceived 'Other(s)'. Very often the Other is 'mainstream culture' or the culture associated with authority and its values, such as anti-drug and anti-hedonism values. It is when these values seem to be being flouted that the media are likely to resort to discursive strategies that amplify the threat and generate a moral panic about the risks to the moral and social order, not just to the young people themselves.

4

MORAL PANIC ABOUT MUGGING

Probably the next most famous account of a moral panic after S. Cohen's *Folk Devils and Moral Panics* (1972/80) is the book by Stuart Hall and his colleagues at Birmingham CCCS, *Policing the Crisis: Mugging, the State and Law and Order* (1978). It has been widely debated, usually in terms critical of its 'Marxist' perspective, or as an example of an 'interest theory' of moral panics (as we discussed in Chapter 1). Critics also accuse it of playing down the real increase in violent crime in the 1970s and the rational fears this engendered, particularly among the working class, who were often its victims (cf. Waddington 1986). However, I believe that the originality of the work lay not so much in its use of Marxist thories concerning capitalism and the state, but in its imaginative decoding of media narratives and its detailed analysis of the 'signification spiral' – a process of publicly signifying issues and problems which is intrinsically escalating. It is the way in which the Birmingham researchers 'decode' the discourses used by the mass media and show how these create a particular impression of moral decline that is most valuable for our study of *moral* panics. In other words, we are not so much interested here in whether certain crimes were

increasing, nor whether people's fears were proportionate (feelings of fear are difficult to investigate when we have only press
reports to go on). The study will be examined for the lessons it
can teach about the decoding of signifying practices as a form of
discourse analysis, in this case media discourses that took the
form of a 'signification spiral' amplifying episodes of 'deviant'
behaviour to create a sense of increasing risk.

The authors of *Policing the Crisis* began their analysis of 'the
social production of news' by making clear that the media do not
simply and transparently report events which are 'naturally'
newsworthy *in themselves*. 'News' has to be seen as the end-product
of a complex process, which begins with a systematic sorting and
selecting of events and topics according to a socially constructed
set of categories. There is a professional ideology of what constitutes 'good news' − the journalist's sense of 'news values' − which
structures the process. The primary news value relates to an
orientation to items which are 'out of the ordinary', breaching our
'normal' expectations about social life. However, there are a
number of other key news values in addition to extraordinariness,
such as: events which concern elite persons or collectivities;
events which are dramatic; events which can be personalized so as
to point up the essentially human characteristics of humour,
sadness, sentimentality, etc.; events which have negative consequences; and events which are part of, or can be made to appear
part of, an existing newsworthy theme (Hall *et al.* 1978: 52).
Another important element in the social construction of news
involves the presentation of the item to an *assumed* audience in
terms which the presenters judge will make it comprehensible to
that audience:

> If the world is not to be represented as a jumble of random
> and chaotic events, then they must be identified (i.e. named,
> defined, related to other events known to the audience), and
> assigned to a social context (i.e. placed within a frame of
> meanings familiar to the audience). This process − identifica-
> tion and contextualisation − is one of the most important
> through which events are 'made to mean' by the media. An

event only 'makes sense' if it can be located within a range of
known social and cultural identifications.

(Hall *et al.* 1978: 54)

One background assumption to this process of making an
event intelligible is that of the *consensual* nature of society: 'the
process of *signification* – giving social meanings to events – *both
assumes and helps to construct society as a "consensus"'* (ibid.: 54; italics
in original) So when events are mapped by the media into frameworks of meanings and interpretation, it is assumed that any
social and cultural divisions are contained within that more
fundamental consensus, and that we all know how to use these
frameworks. The most important significance of the framing and
interpretative function of news presentation is that the media are
often presenting information that is outside the direct experience
of their audience, and this 'problematic reality' breaches
commonly held expectations and so is threatening to a society
based around expectations of consensus, order and routine. The
media map these problematic events within conventional understandings by defining *what* significant events are taking place and
offering interpretations of *how* to understand them.

The next step in the analysis was to explain how the routine
structures of news production tend to reproduce the definitions
of the powerful. The explanation offered was that the practical
pressures of constantly working against the clock and meeting
the professional demands of impartiality and objectivity, and so
being dependent on authoritative statements from 'accredited
sources', combine to produce a systematically structured *over-
accessing* by the media of those in powerful and privileged
institutional positions. These powerful institutional representatives become the *primary definers* of topics. The primary definers
tend to establish the primary interpretative framework of the
topic – the 'inferential structure' (Lang and Lang 1955); even
arguments against the primary interpretation have to insert
themselves into its definition of 'what is at issue'. According to
the Birmingham researchers, this structured relationship
between the powerful institutionally based primary definers and

the media ensures that the dominant ideas or ideologies are constantly reproduced.

However, the cycle of ideological reproduction is not due to a conspiracy, nor is it mechanical and automatic. It is subject to the *transformation* which the media themselves perform on the 'raw materials', even if this is contained within certain ideological limits. Each newspaper may differently appropriate the criteria of selectivity, particularly in view of their sense of their own audience. They will also vary in their transformation of the material in keeping with the particular personality of the newspaper and its version of the language of the public to whom it is addressed. The newspapers' translation of the statements of the primary definers into a public idiom not only makes them more available to the uninitiated; it also invests them with popular force and resonance, naturalizing them within the horizon of understandings of the various publics.

The example given to illustrate this process was a story in the *Daily Mirror* of 14 June 1973 about the Chief Inspector of Constabulary's Annual Report, in which he claimed that 'the increase in violent crimes in England and Wales had aroused justifiable public concern'. The *Mirror* translated the Chief Inspector's concern with rising violent crime amongst the young into a more dramatic, more connotative and more popular form. Its news headline was simply: 'AGGRO BRITAIN: "Mindless violence" of the bully boys worries top policeman'. The Report was given dramatic news value and its staid officialese transposed into more newsworthy rhetoric. It also inserted the statement into the stock of popular imagery, including the usage created by the paper's own previous coverage of 'aggro' football hooligans and Skinhead gangs.

> This transformation into a public idiom thus gives the item an external public reference and validity in images and connotations already sedimented in the stock of knowledge which the paper and its public share. The importance of this external public reference point is that it serves to *objectify* a public issue. That is, the publicising of an issue in the media can give

it a more 'objective' status as a *real* (valid) issue of public concern than would be the case had it remained as merely a report made by experts and specialists. Concentrated media attention confers the status of high public concern on issues which are highlighted; these generally become understood by everyone as the 'pressing issues of the day'. This is part of the media's agenda-setting function. Setting agendas also has a reality-confirming effect.

(Hall *et al.* 1978: 62)

A reverse process to that in which the media translates dominant definitions into an (assumed) public idiom is that where the press is to be found *taking on the public voice* and claiming to be speaking for the public. This taking the public voice, claiming to articulate what the 'moral majority' think, aims to enlist public legitimacy for views which the newspaper itself is expressing, and represents the media in their most campaigning role. These press representations of public opinion are often then enlisted by those in power as 'impartial evidence' of what the public wants. At this point the 'spiral of amplification' is particularly tight. It is not so much that there is a perfect ideological closure in thinking about the subject, but rather that alternative viewpoints are difficult to insert on terms other than those set by the dominant framework. On some controversial issues, where there is a powerfully institutionalized and articulate alternative 'voice', it may be possible to shift the discourse on to new ground, but usually the terms determining what is 'reasonable', 'rational' and not 'extreme' are well established. This is particularly evident in a field such as crime.

In the case of the production of crime news the media are heavily dependent on the primary definers – the institutions of crime control, such as the police, Home Office spokespersons and the courts. The police can claim a double expertise in the 'war against crime', based on professional training and personal experience. Journalists are dependent on them as their major source of information and are reluctant to lose their trust. The Home Office, because it is responsible to Parliament, can claim legitimacy as representing the will of the people. Whilst the judges, with all their panoply of ceremonial dignity, have great symbolic status as the guardians of morality and the punishers of offences against the 'collective conscience', as the sociologist Emile Durkheim called this moral basis of social integration. There are few, if any, competing and alternative sources of definition to these authoritative primary definers of crime, which shape the construction of crime stories in their typical formats. As Stuart Hall *et al.* explain:

> This near monopoly situation provides the basis for three typical formats for crime news which together cover most variants of crime stories. First, the report based on police statements about investigations of a particular case – which involve a police reconstruction of the event and details of the action they are taking. Second, the 'state of the war against crime report' – normally based on Chief Constables' or Home Office statistics about current crime, together with an interpretation by the spokesmen of what the bare figures mean – what is the most serious challenge, where there has been most police success, etc. Third, the staple diet of crime reporting – the story based on a court case: some, where the case is held to be especially newsworthy, following the day to day events of the trial; others where just the day of sentencing and especially the judges' remarks are deemed newsworthy; and still others which consist merely of brief summary reports.
>
> (Stuart Hall *et al.* 1978: 69)

The Birmingham researchers applied this analysis to the press coverage of a particular type of crime, 'mugging', over a thirteen-month sample period from August 1972 to August 1973. 'Mugging' broke as a news story because of its extraordinariness. The first publicized case was on 15 August 1972, when an elderly widower was stabbed to death near Waterloo Station. The national press labelled it – borrowing a description offered by a police officer who had recently visited America – 'a mugging gone wrong'. As the *Daily Mirror* (17 August 1972) headline put it: 'As crimes of violence escalate, a word common in the United

States enters the British headlines: Mugging. To our police, it's a frightening new strain of crime.' The *Daily Mirror* described the event on the basis of police information and imaginative recon-struction, and added supporting evidence about an escalation in crimes of violence. They described the man as having been attacked by three young men, who attempted to rob him, and when he fought back he was stabbed. So far as the definition was concerned, the paper commented that the word was American and derived from such phrases as 'attacking a *mug*: an easy victim' (ibid.). According to the *Mirror*, American police 'describe it as an assault by crushing the victim's head or throat in an armlock or to rob with any degree of force, with or without a weapon' (ibid.). There then followed statistics on increases in crimes of this nature in America and on the London underground. The implication was spelled out by the *Mirror*: 'slowly mugging is coming to Britain' (ibid.). A whole set of connotations about the dark side of American city life was conjured up, with the usual implication that America represented the future for Britain, unless drastic action was taken to stem the tide.

A lone liberal voice attempted to question whether 'mugging' was a new strain of crime. Louis Blom-Cooper QC, in *The Times*, expressed the view that:

> There is nothing new in this world: and mugging, apart from its omission from the Oxford English Dictionary, is not a new phenomenon. Little more than 100 years ago there occurred in the streets of London an outcrop of robbery with violence. It was called 'garrotting', which was an attempt to choke or strangle the victim of a robbery.
>
> (*The Times*, 20 October 1972)

Interestingly, some time before the police had taken up the mugging label, the Metropolitan Police Commissioner, in his Annual Report of 1964, commenting on the 30 per cent increase in 'robberies or assaults with intent to rob', explicitly referred to the fact that 'London has always been the scene of robberies from further back than the days of highwaymen and footpads' (quoted in Hall *et al.* 1978: 5). And despite the subsequent use of the term by police, judges and the Home Office, no legal category of 'mugging' as a crime exists, and the statistics had to be based on lumping together 'robberies' from the person or 'assaults with intent to rob', or other similar and conventional charges.

It is futile to dwell too long on the question of definitions and statistics (Stuart Hall and colleagues looked in detail at the question), as the main point of the analysis is to show how the application of the label 'mugging', and the construction of stories about it, can be shown to have led to a moral panic. In other words, we are interested in how descriptions of a few events could carry such connotations that people felt there was a new and widespread threat to the moral foundations that held society together.

The months after the first application of the label were marked by mounting press coverage of 'mugging' as an issue. The feature precipitating and sustaining this, and the focus of editorial comment, was the use of 'exemplary' sentences. Young people charged with anything that could loosely be labelled 'mugging' were given severe sentences of imprisonment that even the judges admitted were unprecedented but necessary to stem the tide. The police and politicians took up the campaign, declaring a 'war on mugging'. Soon they were declaring that the war was being won (*Sunday Mirror*, 22 October 1972). However, public anxiety, having been aroused, could not easily be soothed. A public opinion survey in the *Daily Mail* (10 November 1972) reported that 90 per cent of those interviewed wanted stiffer sentences and 70 per cent greater government urgency. And then in March 1973 came the case that brought the issue back into the headlines: the sentencing of three Handsworth youths, one to twenty years' detention and the others to ten years' for assaulting a man on a piece of wasteground, robbing him of 30p and returning to the scene later to renew their assault. In the initial press construction of this news story, the *primary news* focused on the extraordinary factors: the *unprecedented* sentences, the *violence* and the *bizarre* fact that the crime was for 30p. After this the focus shifted, the secondary set of *feature news values* came into play in the follow-up stories. At the level of the professional subculture of journalists it involved a recognition that 'there is more to this than meets the eye'. It is at this point of features in the journalistic discourse that the connection between media processes and the more widely distributed 'lay ideologies' of crime are exposed by the Birmingham CCCS authors.

Among the typifications that appear in the feature articles on 21 March 1973 following up on the Handsworth mugging are the reference to a Mafia-type 'Gang Boss' (a headline in the *Daily Mail*); references to the gang leader's 'West Indian' father and his racial resentment (*Daily Mail* and *Daily Express*); the slum or ghetto – summoning up the ghetto/crime connection elaborated in stories about American muggings; the 'immigrant area' (*Daily Express*). The effect, according to Hall and his colleagues, was that:

> The over-arching 'public image' which dominated the national papers' feature treatment of the Handsworth case was that of the *ghetto* or *new slum*. It was this image which was inserted at the moment when the crime/environment relationship was most pressing, ideologically. The 'transparent' association between crime, race, poverty and housing was condensed into the image of the 'ghetto' but not in any causal formulation. Any further demand for explanation was forestalled by this essentially circular definition – these *were* the characteristics which made up the ghetto. The intial 'problem' – the crime – was thus inserted into a more general 'social problem' where the apparent richness of description and evocation stood in place of analytic connections. The connections which were made – with the death of cities, the problem of immigration, the crisis of law and order – were fundamentally *descriptive* connections. Through the 'public image of the ghetto' we were pushed up the scale where generalised analogy replaced concrete analysis and where the image of the United States as precursor of all our nightmares came back into play. It was a powerful and compelling form of *rhetorical closure*.
>
> (Stuart Hall *et al.* 1978: 118)

Social dislocation of a slightly different kind was stressed in the local Birmingham newspapers. Here the images were of youth without leisure facilities and so a source of danger (a frequent theme in postwar moral panics about youth), and the decline of the traditional family and its associated values and discipline. The Birmingham *Sunday Mercury* suggested that crime was the price that had to be paid for forsaking these family values and poor housing and poverty need not have led to crime if a proper home with 'mother in her rightful place' had been provided. If the ghetto was an image of urban decay and possibly racial threat for the national press, the appeal to the family as an image of moral decline appeared prominently in the local press, according to the Birmingham analysis.

To summarize this analysis of the construction of news, it suggests that journalists are dependent on primary definers in the institutions for the initial reporting of news events, and then on lay ideologies in the feature follow-up articles that seek to explain the causes and wider social relevance of the events. One of the organizing themes or condensing images that seems to crop up frequently is that of the nightmare images of the 'dark side' of America that have been so deeply implanted by popular culture portrayals – from Hollywood films to reports dwelling on the violence of American inner city ghettos. Another theme was that of threats to the family and its values as a source of stability and a buttress against crime among the working class.

Before looking at the Birmingham Centre's more detailed account of the lay ideologies, it is worth mentioning another valuable source of data from the media that they analysed: letters to the editor. This is an aspect of the press that had rarely been touched on by British sociologists of the media up to that time. Letter columns are an interesting phenomenon because they appear to give an impression of balance and democratic access to the media; they are where 'ordinary folk' seem to be able to join in the public conversation and debate in the public sphere. Of course, they are subject to selection by the letters editor, and it is often the case that influential or powerful spokespersons are given privileged access, but editors do like letters that appear to speak from personal experience.

The researchers categorized the letters into 'liberals', 'traditionalists' and 'radicals'. The overwhelming majority of the letters printed in the national press on the muggings issue were from 'traditionalists', and it is the content of those letters, as well as the feature articles, that supplied many of the elements of what Hall and his colleagues identified as the dominant 'traditionalist consensus' and ideology. This had a number of linked components. Prominent among them was the notion of *respectability* as a key value. It touched on 'Protestant' values such as thrift, self-discipline and living the decent life, connected to ideas of self-help, self-reliance and conformity to established social standards. For the working class it was important in relation to work, poverty and crime. For the 'respectable' working class, as distinct from the 'rough', loss of respectability was associated with loss of occupation and with poverty, which often led to crime or moral misconduct. Overarching these social images and holding them together was a sense of the national (English) character, as being fundamentally 'commonsensical', with implications of pragmatism verging on anti-intellectualism. These images cohered in a vista of stability − of solid bedrock and unchanging habits and virtues that remained 'forever England'.

However, a number of specific social changes had combined to undercut some of the crucial supports to this set of images, producing social anxiety and a sense of increasing risk that was particularly acute for some classes, especially sections of the working class and the lower middle class. One change was the growth in affluence in the postwar boom in production, associated with attitudes of materialism, hedonism and permissiveness, which were at odds with the traditional Protestant ethic values. This was disturbing for the lower middle class, who did not benefit and who had invested everything in those virtues of thrift, respectability and moral discipline. They were especially resentful of young people who seemed to flout those values. There were also changes producing social anxiety among the traditional communities of the respectable working class, such as the break-up of old neighbourhoods and family networks that had exercised informal controls over the young. These developments were collapsed into three overlapping images of unsettledness: youth, affluence and permissiveness. Many older people experienced social anxiety as a sense of resentment and powerlessness and either engaged in moral 'clean-up' campaigns if they were middle class (e.g. Mrs Mary Whitehouse's 'Clean-Up TV' campaign) or directed their hostility against 'outsiders', immigrants and 'alien' influences such as aspects of American popular culture. The alien forces became the 'folk devil' or scapegoat, the bearer of all the social anxieties, the reverse image of all that was familiar and virtuous. As Stuart Hall *et al.* put it:

> The 'mugger' was such a Folk Devil; his form and shape accurately reflect the content of the fears and anxieties of those who first imagined, and then actually discovered him: young, black, bred in, or arising from the 'breakdown of social order' in the city; threatening the traditional peace of the streets, the security of movement of the ordinary respectable citizen; motivated by naked gain, a reward he could come by, if possible, without a day's honest toil; his crime, the outcome of a thousand occasions when adults and parents had failed to correct, civilise and tutor his wilder impulses; impelled by an even more frightening need for 'gratuitous violence', an inevitable result of the weakening of moral fibre in family and society, and the general collapse of respect for discipline and authority. In short, the very token of 'permissiveness', embodying in his every action and person, feelings and values that were the opposite of those decencies and restraints which make England what she is. He was a sort of personification of all the positive social images – only *in reverse*: black on white. It would be hard to construct a more appropriate Folk Devil.
>
> (Stuart Hall *et al.* 1978: 161–2)

In concluding this discussion of the account of the moral panic about mugging in *Policing the Crisis*, it is worth reiterating that we have chosen to focus on its analysis of media texts in relation to public opinion, professional journalistic practices, lay ideologies, and social anxieties. It is here that its most fruitful contribution to the study of moral panics is to be found, rather than in seeing it as an explanation in terms of the relation of a moral panic to a 'crisis of the state', or as an example of an 'elite-engineered' crisis (as implied by Goode and Ben-Yehuda 1994).

The issue of 'mugging' did not disappear from the media, although it did become routinized and lost some of its character as a sudden and all-consuming panic after the period discussed in *Policing the Crisis*. It took its place featuring as part of a regular campaign against rising crime. However, it showed that it could flair up as a symbol of a 'race' problem, as when the Commissioner of the Metropolitan Police, Sir Paul Condon, claimed in July 1995 that most muggings in the capital were committed by young black men. His private letter to forty black community leaders inviting them to meet with him to talk about the problem was leaked to the press, which greeted it with headlines such as 'Top policeman shatters taboo: Condon acts on black crime' (*Daily Express*, 7 July 1995) and 'Met Chief breaks taboo to reveal most muggers are black' (*The Daily Telegraph*, 7 July 1995). The *Guardian*, as in the 1970s, took the typical liberal line of seeking a 'balance' (as Stuart Hall *et al.* (1978) described it), pointing out that:

> The most authoritative study, the Home Office's British Crime Survey, reveals that nationally the majority of white victims of mugging were assaulted by white offenders and black victims by black assailants. London will be different. We know that muggers are drawn disproportionately from unemployed, poor, badly educated and badly housed young people. Undoubtedly a disproportionate number of young, unemployed, poor, badly housed and badly educated people in London are black. That does not mean most young black people are muggers. Only a small proportion are involved. Nor does it mean that young black people are more likely to mug people than young white people. All the evidence suggests it is social and economic circumstances – rather than ethnic origins – which are the more important determinants. People

of similar ages, living in similar social conditions and with
similar incomes, have roughly the same offending rates.
(The *Guardian*, leader article, 8 July 1995)

Stuart Hall *et al.* had pointed out in their 1978 study that the
liberal ideology represented in the *Guardian* claimed to 'strike a
balance' but was always contained within the limits set by the
current dominant ideology, and this was borne out in the
Guardian's leader on this occasion. Fearing the accusation of
'political correctness', which was then a criticism against liberals,
it concluded by warning black leaders not to quibble about the
statistics but to meet with Sir Paul, noting that 'one of the best
reports on mugging' showed that many of the muggers were
'style-obsessed young blacks intent on buying designer clothes to
achieve increased street credibility' (the *Guardian*, 8 July 1995).
The dominant ideology set the bounds within which the problem
could be addressed and, as it had been inflected by the success of
1980s Thatcherism and Reaganism in reasserting values of free-
market capitalism and individual enterprise, it ruled out more
radical structural changes that might entail increased public
spending and the redistribution of wealth to help the unemployed, poor, badly educated and badly housed people. Instead, as
the *Guardian* leader mentioned, Sir Paul was being accused of
seeking to appease militants in his own ranks who were angry
that he had previously acted against racism within his force and
had devoted his first speech to equal opportunities, so that he had
become known in the service as 'PC Condon – Politically Correct
Condon'.

If we were to apply the Birmingham analysis to such contemporary articles we might begin by noting that 'political
correctness' is a label that conservatives in America used as part of
their backlash against liberals, particularly 'intellectuals', who it
was claimed had 'gone too far' in seeking to change the traditional, or 'natural', social order, in which those who were white,
male, rich and powerful merited their success. In Britain the label
of 'political correctness' has the added stigma of suggesting not
only intellectualism usurping 'common sense', but also that the

ideas so labelled are 'foreign'. If anything has changed since the moral panic about mugging in the 1970s, it is not that the phenomenon is no longer regarded as the latest *new* import from America, but that the contending ideologies about it, both liberal and conservative, have taken on more American characteristics – as indicated by the use of terms such as 'political correctness' and 'zero tolerance'.

5

MORAL PANICS ABOUT SEX AND AIDS

We have seen that moral panics can be analysed from a number of different perspectives and that it may be a sensible tactic to adopt insights from each of these in an eclectic manner or to combine them where appropriate, depending on the particular type of moral panic being analysed. Thus, moral panics concerning youth have been analysed from the perspective of subcultures, whilst other studies adopt a social psychological perspective derived from disaster studies and other forms of collective behaviour. In this chapter we will focus on processes of representation and on mapping the discourses which the mass media use to construct a view of the events which gives rise to a sense of increasing risk and possibly moral panics, particularly panics about sexuality. A common theoretical feature of sociological analyses of these moral panics about sexuality is the focus on discourses that regulate sexuality and defend a notion of what is 'normal', 'natural' and so 'moral'. Following Foucault (1979), many of these analyses argue that we need to recognize that the image of the threatened and vulnerable family is a central motif in modern society. Familial ideology is obliged to fight a continual rearguard action in order to disavow the social and sexual diversity of a culture which can never be adequately pictured in the traditional guise of the family of cohabiting parents and children – a situation which is now occupied by only a minority of citizens at any given moment. However, familial ideology is not the only factor that might explain moral panics about sexuality. Foucault (1979) and Weeks (1985) have attempted to explain why sex itself is so important, so separate from the other human 'attributes' in modern society. They conclude that it is because our culture believes that sex speaks the truth about ourselves, that it expresses the essence of our being, and that it is for these reasons that it has become the subject of controversies and panics. Any concern about the social order is inevitably projected on to this essence, and through this sexuality becomes both an anxious metaphor and a subject of social control. Consequently, moral panics about sex are increasingly the most frequent and have the most serious repercussions in modern society.

AIDS

Susan Sontag's book *Illness and Metaphor* (1983), which was written following her treatment for cancer and analyses the imagery surrounding cancer and tuberculosis, has been influential in developing an understanding of how illness such as these and AIDS are constructed in the popular imagination. She identifies the metaphorical uses to which illness and disease may be put in 'making sense' of prevailing social arrangements (a theme also developed by Foucault in *The Birth of the Clinic*, 1973). An important consideration is the way in which a succession of illnesses are given a moralistic meaning that stigmatizes the victim as a pariah or social deviant. This moralizing process is increasingly accomplished through representations in the mass media.

Early reporting and newspaper comment on AIDS provide many examples of this process. In the British press, the columnist John Junor, writing in the *Sunday Express* (24 February 1985), wrote: 'If AIDS is not an Act of God with consequences just as frightful as fire and brimstone, then just what is it?' And a more elliptical leader in a similar vein in *The Times* (3 November 1984) claimed: 'Many members of the public are tempted to see in AIDS some sort of retribution for a questionable lifestyle, but AIDS of course is a danger not only to the promiscuous nor only to homosexuals.' Other papers used the device of reported speech and allusion to the views of third parties to make similar references. The *Sun* (7 February 1985), for example, carried the headline 'AIDS is the wrath of God, says vicar' and the *Daily Telegraph* (3 May 1983) used quotation marks to similar effect: '"Wages of sin" A deadly toll.' Newspaper reporting also tended to differentiate between so-called 'innocent' and 'guilty' victims of the syndrome. Deaths of those who contracted the disease as a result of 'illicit' or 'morally unacceptable' practices (gays, bisexuals, prostitutes, drug users) were presented more negatively in the media than deaths of those infected as a result of blood transfusions or other accidental factors. In a headline story involving a schoolchild with AIDS, the *Daily Express* (25 September 1985) asked: 'AIDS: Why must the innocent suffer?' Even animals being used to test a possible cure were portrayed as 'innocent' and more deserving of sympathy than the 'guilty' victims: 'Torture of innocents: Chimps in "sex plague" tests' (*Sunday Mirror*, 4 December 1983). Another feature of reporting in the early 1980s, at least until the National Union of Journalists issued guidelines after an enquiry in 1984, was to refer to AIDS as the 'gay plague' (e.g. *Daily Telegraph*, 2 May 1983; *The Observer*, 26 June 1983; *Sun*, 2 May 1983; *Daily Mirror*, 2 May 1983). Finally, there was a constant tendency to exaggerate the numbers of people involved by extrapolating from clinical data to the wider population or by projecting forward previous rates of increase on the assumption that these are certain to be sustained. For example, a clinical study of gay men at a clinic at St Mary's Hospital, London, showing that 12 per cent of symptom-free clinic attenders had lymphocyte abnormalities characteristic of AIDS and 5 per cent also had anergy, the index combination of defects seen in AIDS, was reported under the headline: 'Thousands of British gays have symptoms of AIDS' (*The Observer*, 7 August 1983). Meanwhile the Royal College of Nursing issued a prediction that there would be 1 million cases in Britain by 1991; this was reported verbatim or as a rate of one in fifty by *The Times*, the *Sun*, the *Daily Mirror*, the *Daily Express* and the *Daily Star* (10 January 1985) (Aggleton and Homans 1988). The projections were made on the basis of assuming the continuation of the exponential growth rate of the early years of the disease, without questioning whether all the factors would remain the same, especially whether there might be changes in behaviour limiting the spread of infection.

As we saw in considering S. Cohen's pioneering study of moral panics, the mass media provide 'a main source of information about the normative contours of a society . . . about the boundaries beyond which one should not venture and about the shapes the devil can assume' (S. Cohen 1972: 17). The mass media, it is alleged, construct 'pseudo-events' according to the dictates of an unwritten moral agenda which constitutes newsworthiness. Thus, 'rumour . . . substitutes for news when institutional channels fail' (ibid.: 154), and in ambiguous situations 'rumours should be viewed not as forms of distorted or pathological communication; they make sociological sense as co-operative improvisations, attempts to reach a meaningful collective interpretation of what happened by pooling available resources' (ibid.: 154).

In an important essay on AIDS, Jeffrey Weeks draws heavily on moral panic theory, explaining how its mechanisms 'are well known':

> the definition of a threat to a particular event (a youthful 'riot', a sexual scandal); the stereotyping of the main characters in the mass media as particular species of monsters (the prostitute as 'fallen woman', the paedophile as 'child molester'); a spiralling escalation of the perceived threat, leading to a taking up of absolutist positions and the manning of moral barricades; the emergence of an imaginary solution – in tougher laws, moral isolation, a symbolic court action; followed by the subsidence of the anxiety, with its victims left to endure the new proscription, social climate and legal penalties.
>
> (Weeks 1985: 45)

Dennis Altman also discusses AIDS in terms of moral panic, but relates the form the panic takes to local and national factors. Thus:

> the Australian panic is not only a product of homophobia but is also tied to the . . . belief that they can insulate themselves from the rest of the world through rigid immigration and quarantine laws [and] a less sophisticated understanding and acceptance of homosexuality than exists in the United States.
>
> (Altman 1986: 186)

Calls for draconian legislation in such disparate societies as West Germany and Sweden lead him to conclude that 'the link between Aids and homosexuality had the potential for unleashing panic and persecution in almost every society' (Altman 1986: 187).

Simon Watney (1987) argues that whilst such analyses have a certain usefulness they also reveal the inadequacy of the concept of moral panic to his main interest, which is the overall ideological policing of sexuality, especially in matters of representations. Watney describes his book *Policing Desire: Pornography, Aids and the Media* as being about representation, and as being written in the belief that we can only ultimately conceive of ourselves and one another in relation to the circulation of available images in any given society. He quotes approvingly the statement of Richard Dyer:

> A major legacy of the social political movements of the Sixties and Seventies has been the realisation of the importance of representation. The political chances of different groups in society – powerful or weak, central or marginal – are crucially affected by how they are represented, whether in legal and parliamentary discourse, in educational practices, or in the arts. The mass media in particular have a crucial role to play, because they are a centralised source of definitions of what people are like in any given society. How a particular group is represented determines in a very real sense what it can do in society.
>
> (Dyer 1982: 43)

Watney criticizes moral panics theory because, he claims, it is always obliged to contrast 'representation' to the arbitration of 'the real', and is therefore unable to develop a full theory concerning the operations of ideology within all representational systems:

> Moral panics seem to appear and disappear, as if representation were not the site of permanent ideological struggle over the meaning of signs. A particular 'moral panic' merely marks the site of the current front-line in such struggles. We do not in fact witness the unfolding of discontinuous and discrete 'moral panics', but rather the mobility of ideological confrontation across the entire field of public representations, and in particular those handling and evaluating the meanings of the human body, where rival and incompatible forces and values are involved in a ceaseless struggle to define supposedly universal 'human' truths.
>
> (Watney 1987: 42)

In making this criticism, Watney is not so much denying that certain episodes constitute moral panics. It is rather that he wishes to broaden the discussion to place the panic over AIDS within the broader framework of ideological contestation about how certain groups are represented by the mass media as threats to the cohesion of a unified 'general public'. He maintains that the mass media use a mode of address to their audience which constructs them as a unified 'general public' with shared values and characteristics:

> It is the central ideological business of the communications industry to retail ready-made pictures of 'human' identity, and thus recruit individual consumers to identify with them in a fantasy of collective mutual complementarity. Whole sections of society, however, cannot be contained within this project, since they refuse to dissolve into the larger mutualities required of them. Hence the position, in particular, though in different ways, of both blacks and gay men, who are made to stand outside the 'general public', inevitably appearing as

threats to its internal cohesion. This cohesion is not 'natural', but the result of the media industry's modes of address – targeting an imaginary national 'family' unit which is both white and heterosexual. All apparent threats to this key object of individual identification will be subject to the kinds of treatment which [Stanley] Cohen and his followers describe as moral panics. . . . We are not, in fact, living through a distinct, coherent and progressing 'moral panic' about AIDS. Rather, we are witnessing the latest variation in the spectacle of the defensive ideological rearguard action which has been mounted on behalf of 'the family' for more than a century.

(Watney 1987: 43)

Not only do the mass media attempt to address their audience as a unified, natural 'subject' (addressing them individually as 'normal', 'healthy-minded', 'right-thinking', commonsensical subjects), Watney alleges that newspapers in particular tend to construct 'an ideal audience of national family units, surrounded by the threatening spectacle of the mad, the foreign, the criminal and the perverted' (1987: 84). Hence:

The Press is therefore heavily dependent upon the very categories which it ceaselessly offers up as exemplary signs of 'the breakdown of law and order' or simply 'the disgusting' or 'the depraved'. Scandal serves the purpose of exemplary exclusion in newspaper discourse, and is the central means whereby readers find themselves reassured and reconciled as 'normal', law-abiding citizens.

(Watney 1987: 84)

Watney uses the example of press linking of royalty, the family, the nation, and the threat of AIDS from homosexuality to illustrate the way in which we can map this type of discursive formation. The *Star* newspaper published a story running to three pages under the front page banner headline: 'GAY LOVERS ON ROYAL YACHT; Shock as Fergie and Andrew plan honeymoon.' The story, which appeared before the wedding of Princess Andrew and Sarah Ferguson, stated that:

> Gay sailors have been serving the Queen and Prince Philip aboard the Royal Yacht Britannia, the *Star* can exclusively reveal. The scandal came to light when steward Keith Jury told his wife he'd been having an affair with a Royal Marine Bandsman.
>
> (*Star*, 3 July 1986)

Watney suggests that the shock impact of the story rested on the implied association of the overlap of narratives about homosexuality, AIDS and the monarchy. Although AIDS was not mentioned, Watney maintains that it was the missing yet crucial term which 'explains' the otherwise inexplicable length of the story. The mere fact of gay sex is held to be dangerous for other people, not as a temptation to imitate, but possibly as a hazard to life itself, and certainly as a threat to the image of purity and idealized family life of the Royal Family (soon to be shattered by real heterosexual scandals!). Watney describes this in terms of a mapping operation by which human subjects are represented within a discursive formation that links together royalty, family, nation and sexuality in such a way as to render homosexuality as deviant and dangerous – requiring social regulation either through medicalization or incarceration:

> The press is thus radically prescriptive. It presents the world which it would like to see in the likeness of an imaginary national past, just as it defends and justifies its rejection of what it cannot acknowledge in the present by recourse to imaginary futures. And when the contour maps of sexuality and national identity are obliged to duplicate one another, it is homosexuality which is squeezed out first. This mapping operation can only accept one primary distinction between human subjects – the physical opposition male/female. Other divisions which threaten to disrupt and invalidate this picture are ruthlessly stigmatised. Thus the hospital ward joins the prison cell as the 'proper' site of homosexuality, offering a limited and closely supervised window onto the forbidden and unknown, and finding there what it consistently warned against all along – corruption and contagion – the just desserts of those who are

thought to reject the national family. In a situation where sexuality and gender are clearly held as the primary determinations of 'character', in a discourse of 'real men' and 'real women', gay men and lesbians are serious offenders. Thus the press 'knows' what its readers are like, in relation to the pivotal roles of family life – 'mums', 'dads', 'kids', even 'pets', which act out all the other roles 'in little' as it were. All these characters have regularly coded appearances, inflected by class, and their combinations are equally predictable in advance, constituted in a continuum of expectations which stretches from cartoons and gossip columns through regular sections on gardening, sports, finance, fashion, and so on. Homosexuality can only enter this space as an intrusion, just as gay culture in all its forms will be given the spurious unity of a criminal environment, an infernal and bestial domain which is virtually non-human.

(Watney 1987: 86)

Circulation wars between the British tabloid newspapers in the 1980s led them to feature ever more gruesome stories about AIDS, and this escalation certainly led to an air of panic about morals being undermined by 'deviants' (S. Cohen's 'folk devils'), which, despite Watney's hesitations, seems to merit the label of a 'moral panic'. The *Sun* ran a story bringing together religion, the family, homosexuality and AIDS, under the heading: 'I'D SHOOT MY SON IF HE HAD AIDS, Says Vicar! He would pull trigger on rest of his family.' The piece featured the Rev. Robert Simpson, who 'vowed yesterday that he would take his teenage son to a mountain and shoot him if the boy had the deadly disease AIDS' (*Sun*, 14 October 1985). The vicar was pictured holding a shotgun to his son's head. The coverage managed to combine some of the most potent images of threats to normal life: family breakdown, infanticide, teenage sexuality, homosexuality and contagious disease. The Rev. Simpson was reported to have said 'he would ban all practising homosexuals, who are most in danger of catching AIDS, from taking normal communion. If it continues it will be like the Black Plague. It could wipe out Britain. Family will be against family' (ibid.).

The Press Council, the official watchdog on press standards in Britain, rejected complaints about the story that it was likely to create irrational fears about AIDS and to encourage discrimination or violence against people with the disease. The Council concluded:

> In this case the *Sun* chose a dramatic way to focus attention on the danger of Aids. Its article was not presented as medical opinion offered by the paper or as a report of medical opinion, but as a report of the strong views held by a clergyman who had already published similar comments in his parish magazine.
>
> (quoted in Watney 1987: 96)

Watney's argument is that homosexuality is constructed by the press as an exemplary and admonitory sign of Otherness, in order to unite sexual and national identifications among readers over and above all divisions and distinctions of class, race and gender. When he turns to the representation of AIDS in broadcasting, he maintains that, given the close relations between the press and broadcasting, it is not surprising that a similar situation obtains, although less so in radio because of its stronger commitment to regionalism. However, he notes that sexuality is subject to a double bind in relation to television, which is regarded as private at the point of viewing but public in its duties and responsibilities – unlike newspapers, which strongly maintain their independence of the state. Television has always been subject to official regulation, especially in relation to questions of obscenity and indecency. The BBC was founded on an assumption 'of cultural homogeneity; not that everybody was the same, but that culture was single and undifferentiated' (Curran and Seaton 1985: 179). Legislation and regulation sustained a 'consensus' orientation which excluded homosexuality. The home was regarded as a site vulnerable to moral danger, with the focus of attention fixed on the possibility of children watching adult programmes – 'adult' in this context usually meaning sexually explicit. Not surprisingly, therefore, for a long time any representation of sexual 'deviance' was either excluded or referred to in a highly coded manner. The various forms of coding included treating homosexuality as a subject of scandal, humour or humanist pathos. Alternatively, coding could involve treating it as a controversial problem in 'current affairs' programmes, which then required balancing contributions from critics, as in the case of the appearance of the 'Clean-Up TV' campaigner Mary Whitehouse when London Weekend Television ran a series of *Gay Life* magazine programmes in 1980 and 1981.

There was some change in broadcasting representations of homosexuals and AIDS when the British Government became convinced that it had to embark on a massive advertising campaign to increase knowledge about AIDS and safer sex practices. It took a long time to reach this decision and Prime Minister Margaret Thatcher is believed to have done so only with great reluctance. Her own Parliamentary Private Secretary, Michael Allison, MP, was a member of the Conservative Family Campaign, which advocated its own solution to AIDS: the isolation of all those infected and the recriminalization of homosexuality. She herself was a great supporter of Clause 28, an amendment to the Local Government Bill introduced in 1987, which forbids local councils and their schools from promoting the acceptability of homosexuality. However, there were strong reasons for going ahead with a campaign, not least the fact that the US Surgeon General Everett Koop, an ultra-conservative supporter of President Reagan, had published a report in October 1986 which painted a doomsday scenario and emphasized the importance of widespread public education. The Government announced to the House of Commons in November 1986 that it was launching a £20 million public education campaign with newspaper advertisements, posters, a leaflet to every home and a radio, television and cinema campaign. Two days after the Commons debate *The Sunday Telegraph* responded with the headline 'AIDS: The new holocaust'. The *Mail on Sunday* reported that it was the greatest danger facing Britain, and *The Sunday Times* ran a picture of the average family – two parents, two teenagers and a baby: 'They all look happy and healthy. But from what we now know about the way the AIDS epidemic is developing, all are potential victims.' The Government's television advertisements were no less ominous. The first featured an exploding mountain, a tombstone on which was chiselled the words AIDS, and a bunch of flowers; the second featured an iceberg. They did not convey much other than that something terrible was going to happen. Doctors at a Southampton hospital conducted a survey on the effectiveness of the advertisements and found that people still had little idea about the illness; one person whose first language was not English had seen the tombstone advertisement and thought that AIDS was associated with the use of pneumatic drills (Garfield 1994). However, the broadcast campaign, linked to the leafleting, did appear to have had some beneficial effects in increasing the level of expressed compassion for people with AIDS and perhaps in forestalling the victimization of homosexuals (see the Independent Television Commission research report, Wober 1991).

The Government's campaign did not completely halt the moral panic about AIDS. Religious leaders were not impressed with the campaign. The Roman Catholic Church disapproved of condom promotion and the Anglicans expressed doubts about the lack of accompanying moral guidance. The Chief Rabbi, Sir Immanuel Jakobovits, thought it 'encourages promiscuity by advertising it'. The Chief Rabbi had his own message: 'Say plainly: Aids is the consequence of marital infidelity, premarital adventures, sexual deviation and social irresponsibility – putting pleasure before duty and discipline' (Garfield 1994). Some newspaper columnists continued to denounce the deviancy and permissiveness that they blamed for the spread of AIDS, and one of them, Digby Anderson, claiming to speak on behalf of the 'moral majority', regretted bitterly that there had not been more of a moral panic about AIDS (quoted in Watney 1987: 45). However, the Government's educational campaign seemed to have taken the steam out of the moral panic and also undercut its own previous attempt, epitomized by Clause 28, to prevent the promotion of positive views of homosexuality. The National Viewers' and Listeners' Association continued to attempt to arouse public opinion against the moral permissiveness represented by AIDS and issued a report, 'Television programmes and

Aids' (1992), which stated: 'We believe that the role of the media in normalising casual sex has been one of the main factors in creating this almost overwhelming and potentially most dangerous problem (Aids).' But by the 1990s this ideological position was less prevalent in the press than it had been in the 1980s. Another reaction from some parts of the press in the early 1990s was against the so-called 'AIDS industry' and an imaginary liberal Establishment for allegedly blurring the distinction between 'deviants' such as homosexuals and drug-takers, whose behaviour exposed them to risk, and 'normal' people, whose sexual behaviour did not present a risk. As the liberal columnist Neal Ascherson put it, when singling out the then editor of *The Sunday Times*, Andrew Neil, as an example of one of the representatives of this position, this was a variant on a hegemonic ideological theme of the 1980s – the populist criticism of a liberal elite who conspired against the 'aspirations of plain folk' and formed cliques described as 'industries' (Ascherson 1993). The so-called 'AIDS industry' was only the latest manifestation, following on from the 'poverty industry', the 'race relations industry, the 'Third World aid industry', the 'social work industry', and the 'Euro-industry' (allegedly devoted to abolishing Parliament and national sovereignty). In each of these cases, according to the populist ideology represented in much of the mass circulation press, the 'natural common sense' and moral healthiness of the majority of plain, ordinary folk was confronted by the machinations of a morally dubious minority. It was by playing on these contrasts that moral outrage was stirred up and sometimes gave rise to a moral panic.

The significance of AIDS for the study of moral panics is the way in which it was given a moral significance that articulated together with certain ideological themes and discourses that were contending for hegemony in the 1980s, particularly those associated with the New Right's efforts to shape a new majority. As Weeks (1985) points out, there have been three main strands in the moral and sexual shifts of the past generation: a partial secularization of moral attitudes, a liberalization of popular beliefs and behaviours, and a greater readiness to accept social, cultural and sexual diversity. The significance of the AIDS crisis has been that it could be used to call into question each of these, and to justify a return to 'normal moral behaviour'. The changes were never accepted by moral conservatives, and since the 1960s there has been a reaction against them in the form of an attempted reassertion of absolute moral values and 'social purity'. In the US a combination of television evangelism, big money and religious fundamentalism combined with New Right political forces to create the so-called 'moral majority'. Although Britain did not provide the same fertile ground for such a social movement, moral entrepreneurs were able to use the national press's interest in populist causes, especially those alleging threats to 'normal' family life from sexual promiscuity or deviance. Just as feminism could be blamed for disrupting traditional demarcations between the sexes, homosexuality could be attacked as a threat to the family and to the health of society. As Weeks puts it:

> There have been many fundamental changes in the past thirty years, but their impact has been uneven and fragmented, producing frustration as well a social progress, new tensions as well as the alleviations of old injustices. Secularization, liberalization, changes in the pattern of relationships have all taken place. But they have left deep residues of anxiety and fear, which Aids as a social phenomenon has fed on and reaffirmed.
>
> (Weeks 1985: 15)

It is within such a context of social change, anxiety and tension that moral entrepreneurs are able to promote a discourse about alleged threats to what is 'normal', 'natural' and moral with regard to sexuality. Where there is a mass-circulation popular press, as in Britain, there are ample possibilities for the amplification of deviance to give rise to a moral panic. Although Britain possessed the mass-circulation popular press conducive to the development of a moral panic about AIDS, it differed from the United States in not having a tradition of strong, grassroots social movements, including a gay and lesbian rights movement that could engage in debate with an opposed viewpoint in the form of the religious New Right. The press in America is accustomed to acting as a local forum, presenting and reporting the opinions of different pressure groups and social movements. In this respect, it might be argued, it is closer to Habermas's (1984) notion of the media as channels for rational communication, than is the British tabloid press, which corresponds more to Debord's (1970) idea of 'society as spectacle', in which the mass media excite and entertain. Perhaps the only compensation is that competition between newspapers means that the intense coverage that can create a panic can also lead to rapid exhaustion of the subject and its replacement with a new topic, especially if rival journalists cast doubt on the reports that gave rise to the panic. An example was the story about the 'angel of death' in Dungavon, Ireland, in September 1995, when hundreds of British and foreign journalists descended on the small town after the parish priest preached a Sunday sermon claiming that a young Englishwoman had infected at least nine of the local men with AIDS in six months. By Monday the panic was such that the local health board had to set up two emergency counselling lines and, 'as every medieval morality play has to have a witch', as the *Guardian* (14 September 1995) put it, it was rumoured that the press were offering £10,000 for the name of the girl. The health authorities soon began to cast doubt on the feasibility of one woman infecting so many men in such a short space of time, and even the priest's bishop and the local mayor were said to be annoyed with the priest. Within a week the story had burned itself out and the hundreds of journalists had departed.

A further conclusion that might be drawn from this discussion of moral panics associated with AIDS is that they illustrate that although moral panics may be episodic, the discourses that construct attitudes to sexuality are deeply interwoven in the cultural fabric of a society. In a 'society of spectacles', such as where there is a national tabloid press in which newspapers vie with each other to shock and outrage readers, the incidence of moral panics may be greater and have a rapid turnover, but the underlying discourse about 'normal' and 'deviant' sexuality is more long-lasting and is part of a wider discursive formation.

6

FAMILY, CHILDREN AND VIOLENCE

RISK

The concept of 'risk' is particularly relevant to the analysis of moral panics connected with the family. Politicians and media commentators have frequently created a signification spiral through moral discourses concerning episodes or trends that they portray as examples of immorality and violence due to family breakdown. A critic within the press, Polly Toynbee, wrote of the dangerous tendency in the 1990s for British politicians to attempt to ride to victory on a moral tide, 'balanced on a wave of fear, surfing on a flood of moral panic' (the *Independent*, 16 November 1996). She asked who would speak words of calm and common sense in the face of this 'fin de siècle hysteria':

> It leaves the electorate in a turmoil of panic: society is out of control, the family done for, children are running wild, schools teach nothing, crime is rampant, respect is dead, the cult of instant gratification is rife. The very word 'moral' now belongs so firmly with the alarmists that it is virtually unusable by anyone else.
>
> (Polly Toynbee, 'Private tolerance and public panic', the *Independent*, 16 November 1996)

And yet, as she points out, people's personal experience is often at odds with this pessimistic picture and the anxieties about being at risk seem to be out of all proportion:

> We live in curiously schizoid times: so much public comment is at variance with most people's private experience. In the real world people are more liberal than ever before. They are less censorious, more open-minded about cohabitation, homosexuality, babies born out of wedlock and divorce than at any time in history. Soap operas tell the story very well. Within families and among communities of friends and colleagues, we are tolerant as never before. Freedom brings more diversity, more choice – but the flip side of freedom is more risk, danger and dislocation.
>
> (Polly Toynbee, 'Private tolerance and public panic', the *Independent*, 16 November 1996)

This point about increasing choice and diversity generating more of a sense of being at risk is crucial to understanding the frequency of moral panics and the part played by politicians and the media in amplifying those anxieties. It can be argued that in some cases politicians and the media have an interest in generating moral panics. The media are competing for audiences and are tempted to sensationalize, personalize and even demonize in their eagerness to attract attention. Politicians may find it easier to focus attention on moral issues than to come up with solutions to some of the more intractable problems, such as lack of education and skills, unemployment, housing conditions, crime and poverty. However, there are good reasons why the family and 'family values' have become the focus for concern. On the one hand, the family is probably all that is left of traditional 'community' in the sociological sense of *Gemeinschaft*. As the German sociologist Tönnies explained:

> All intimate, private and exclusive living together is understood as life in *Gemeinschaft* (community). *Gesellschaft* (society) is public life – it is the world itself. In *Gemeinschaft* (community) with one's family, one lives from birth on bound to it in weal

and woe. One goes into *Gesellschaft* (society) as one goes into
a strange country.
>   (Tönnies 1887/1955: 37: quoted in K. Thompson: 1996: 51)

Communal or family-like ties, according to Tönnies, could also
exist through shared religious beliefs and folkways, particularly
in rural areas. Modernization entails a loosening of such familiar
communal bonds, leaving people with a sense that they are
constantly going into a strange country and being at risk. On the
other hand, the weakening of traditional beliefs about natural
social hierarchies, including the familial hierarchy in which children were taught to obey their fathers and women promised
lifelong obedience to their husbands, increases the sense of risk
concerning children and family relationships.

Two media campaigns illustrate the recurrent moral panic
about the collapse of the family as a cause of multiple ills,
including violence. The first is the campaign about an 'underclass' mounted by *The Sunday Times* in 1989. The second concerns
the *Daily Mail*'s campaign against the Family Homes and
Domestic Violence Bill in 1995. Both newspapers were major
supporters of the New Right ideology combining Thatcherite
neo-liberal economic policies with neo-conservative moralizing.

The thesis of an 'underclass' as a threat to society has a long
history stretching back into the nineteenth century. However, it
took on a new complexion in the 1980s when the blame for
mounting social ills was directed against 'immoral' single
mothers with illegitimate children and living on welfare
payments. The chief proponent of the thesis was the American
political scientist Charles Murray, who in 1981 joined the right-
wing think-tank the Manhattan Institute for Public Policy
Research, and in 1984 published *Losing Ground: American Social
Policy 1950–1980*. His ideas were soon being constantly cited by
supporters of President Ronald Reagan's policies, and even after
the change to a Democratic administration the *US News and World
Report* was still able to cite him as one of the thirty-two men and
women who dominated American policy formulation. In 1989
The Sunday Times brought him over to Britain and commissioned

him to apply his analysis to British society. His subsequent report filled many pages of the newspaper and was accompanied by a front-page news article about his 'findings' and an editorial comment asserting that: 'A monster is being created in our midst and public policy has no desire to confront it' (*The Sunday Times*, 26 November 1989). The article asserted that 'a social tragedy of Dickensian proportions is in the making. . . . The underclass spawns illegitimate children without a care for tomorrow and feeds on a crime rate which rivals the United States. . . . They reject society while feeding off it; they are becoming a lost generation' (ibid.). In line with Murray's recommendations, it advocated the restoration of the fear of 'social stigma' attached to illegitimacy: 'social stigma is an essential ingredient of social order and must, slowly and cumulatively, be restored' (ibid.). Some blame was attached to the churches for failing to provide any moral framework – their leaders 'seem more anxious to peddle politics than preach family values' (ibid.). Apart from urging moral revitalization and stigmatizing mothers with illegitimate children, *The Sunday Times* added to the panic by agreeing with Murray that there were 'no immediate solutions and that the problem will inevitably get worse' (ibid.).

In summary, *The Sunday Times* and Murray were acting as moral entrepreneurs, promoting a moral campaign claiming that the social problems associated with the poor resulted from a decline in moral values, particularly with regard to sex and marriage, and the availability of welfare benefits. These gave rise to illegitimacy, and this leaves sons with no socially responsible role models (i.e. fathers). Such illegitimate children reject conventional values, refuse to work, engage in criminal activities and foul up neighbourhoods. Furthermore, things are going to get worse and there is little that can be done about it in practical terms. The only answer is moral revitalization and the stigmatizing of social outcasts. No space was given to the alternative argument that, frequently, illegitimacy is a symptom, not a cause of problems. Other factors not mentioned include housing and marital problems, the gap between work aspirations and opportunities, racial discrimination, illness, inadequate local services, poor environment, and so on.

A number of other pertinent questions are simply not addressed in this one-sided account, such as whether there are no other sources of role models – the mother's partner in a long-term relationship, working mothers, uncles, cousins, local people and media figures. Furthermore, in order to substantiate Murray's single-factor theory of illegitimacy, he would have to provide statistical evidence that most of the increase in crime and voluntary unemployment was due to illegitimate children. He did not do this, but simply pointed out that illegitimate birth rates had gone up, along with crime, in areas where youth unemployment had increased. Nor did he give any estimate of the size of this underclass; the statistic of 158,500 illegitimate births in 1987 was qualified by the fact that 6 per cent were to couples living in stable relationships, and it is quite probable that many subsequently married that person or someone else. (The crucial missing statistic relates to 'never married' or 'never in a stable relationship'.)

Media styles of presentation have an important bearing on the development of moral panics. In what has become standard journalistic practice, *The Sunday Times* sought to give a 'human interest' or 'personalized' dimension to the pages of rather arid argument by Murray, and so its reporter provided profiles of three 'underclass' families, illustrated with photographs. What the newspaper did not point out was that none of the cases really substantiated the thesis; the nearest it came to such an admission was in a caption which noted that 'the people present a more complex picture than social theory can allow' (26 November 1989). In fact, the people profiled seemed to cling to fairly conventional values and aspirations, despite the hardships they were suffering. They did not match up to Murray's characterization of the underclass's debased values, which he claimed were 'contaminating the life of entire neighbourhoods' (ibid.). The nearest examples among the people interviewed were a father of illegitimate children, who nevertheless had a job and complained about people dirtying the neighbourhood, and a young unemployed man, who wanted to start his own business and had already bought a briefcase in order to look professional.

Despite the disjuncture between the line taken by the newspaper and the more complicated picture presented by the actual cases, the sensational treatment given to Professor Murray's thesis guaranteed that the paper would achieve its objective of stirring up controversy and attracting attention. Since its purchase by Rupert Murdoch, *The Sunday Times* had developed a reputation for making sensationalist disclosures (once even purchasing fake Hitler diaries) and for promoting the New Right ideology associated with Thatcher and Reagan. Its revelations about the threat to society posed by an underclass of immoral social outcasts certainly provoked many responses, as was revealed in the subsequent week's issue. However, the moral campaign had been effectively launched and the efforts of social scientists to point out the oversimplifications in the thesis received much less coverage (see K. Thompson 1989). The Murdoch papers, *The Times* and *The Sunday Times*, continued to spread their moral campaign and its attendant fear tactics in subsequent years. In 1994 *The Sunday Times* invited Charles Murray to return to address 'The Sunday Times British Underclass Forum'. This was preceded by an article by another American, Gertrude Himmelfarb, also under the banner of 'The Sunday Times British Underclass Forum', and proclaimed Murray's thesis to be an established fact. Once again illegitimacy and the failure to stigmatize it featured large in her ideological attack, although a certain contradiction appeared in the argument claiming that there was a lack of morals whilst at the same time implying that it was more a case of moral priorities having changed and there being a new 'original sin':

> As deviancy is normalised, so the normal becomes deviant. The kind of family that has been regarded for centuries as natural and moral is now seen as pathological, concealing behind the facade of respectability the new 'original sin', child abuse.
>
> (*The Sunday Times*, 11 September 1994)

This statement is interesting because it illustrates the ideological character of discourses such as that concerning the underclass

– defining what is deviant or natural. The way in which the discourse constructs its meanings can be decoded to show that its connotations derive from the associated terms it summons up, such as 'illegitimacy', 'monster', 'cut adrift', 'violence', 'American black ghetto', 'welfare dependency', etc. These connotations play on anxieties common in our risk-aware society. Politicians and moral entrepreneurs find allies in sections of the mass media which share their ideological position. Changes in the mass media have increased competition and persuaded even some of the so-called quality newspapers to seek wider popular appeal, and populist moral campaigning is one of the strategies adopted. There has been a growth of 'infotainment' in the media – mixing information with entertainment. An example is the proliferation of tabloid sections in broadsheet papers and colour magazines in almost all papers. *The Sunday Times*'s coverage of Charles Murray's thesis on the underclass appeared in the colour magazine. The other significant development in the press has been the proliferation of opinion columns, possibly at the expense of factual reporting. Columnists are under pressure to write attention-grabbing and controversial pieces, and this often seems to lead to a competition to see who can stir up the most righteous indignation or extreme generalization. For example, since the 1970s *The Sunday Times* and *The Times* have provided increasing space on their centre pages for opinionated columnists. The editorial leaders have tended to echo the same opinions. There is also a tendency for the different media to refer to each other and so create a common news-opinion agenda. So, the prominent columnist on *The Times*, Janet Daley, could base a column on a *Panorama* television programme about the effects of family breakdown whilst at the same time maintaining that the programme's citing of research findings was 'largely superfluous for the great mass of people who have always sworn that there would be a day of reckoning' (*The Times*, 10 February 1994). The successful columnist seems to believe that the analysis of detailed statistics, along with qualified and balanced arguments, would be too boring and that readers prefer their columnists to resemble Old Testament prophets restating God-given Truth.

The second example fits this bill perfectly, as it involved the *Daily Mail's* right-wing columnist, the Oxford theologian William Oddie, and the Conservative Government's Family Homes and Domestic Violence Bill in 1995. The Bill, which was designed to protect unmarried victims of domestic violence by strengthening their property rights as legally recognized 'cohabitants', enjoyed all-party support and was proceeding through Parliament unopposed. Then William Oddie used his column to paint a lurid picture of its likely consequences, proclaiming that the Bill threatened to sabotage the institution of marriage. He described it as a 'nightmare scenario' (*Daily Mail*, 23 October 1995). When a group of Conservative backbench MPs was roused to confront the Bill's sponsor, the Lord Chancellor, another *Daily Mail* columnist, John Torode, supplied a profile of him, asking: 'How does Lord Mackay find himself on the outer fringes of permissiveness, fighting against his own backbenchers for legislation which infuriates those who look with distress at the breakdown of the family' (*Daily Mail*, 27 October 1995).

The Lord Chancellor's department tried to dismiss as 'scare stories' the claims about the effects of the Bill, but the moral panic was already underway. Within a few days of mounting its campaign, the *Daily Mail* was announcing in its front page headline: 'Live-in lovers Bill is shelved – Climbdown by Mackay after Mail warns that new law would sabotage marriage' (27 October 1995). Another headline gave the impression that it was gays who had set out to destroy the family and had pressured the Lord Chancellor's advisors: 'They listened to gay groups instead of family campaigners' (ibid.). The not-so-coded message, once again, was that social deviants were trying to undermine or reverse the natural moral order based on the family, and this was luridly portrayed as a 'nightmare scenario'.

CHILDREN AT RISK

The various elements of the 'threat to moral values' discourse are now so well established that it is not necessary for the media to list them all for a moral panic to be created. As the coded elements are linked in chains, it is enough to mention just one or two for the others to be summoned up immediately. This is the case where a single event gives rise to a moral panic by being fitted into the pre-established discourse. The event can then crystallize all the associated fears that give rise to panic. A famous example is that of the murder of 2-year-old James Bulger by two young boys. Thus, when *The Sunday Times* ran an editorial leader article on 'The brutality of Britain', it stated:

> The British have sensed for some time that violent crime was gnawing at the edges of the country's social fabric and that those in authority seemed powerless to stop its relentless progress. But it has taken one particular murder to crystallise the country's fears, encapsulate the concern and encourage people to ask aloud what kind of nation we are becoming: the brutal abduction of two-year-old James Bulger, who was led off by two other children. It is the world of the video nasty brought to reality.
>
> (*The Sunday Times*, 21 February 1993)

It went on to refer to 'the social anarchy and squalor of today's "sink" estates, inhabited by a largely white underclass, which has come to resemble in crime, violence, illegitimacy, welfare dependency and general hopelessness the black ghettos of urban America' (ibid.). This was followed by reference to the core element of the Murray thesis:

> The social controls of the community also fail to operate when the most common family type is the single-parent mother, the father long gone. Not only do youngsters – particularly young boys – have no father-figure in the family; there are almost no worthwhile male role-models in the whole community.
>
> (*The Sunday Times*, 21 February 1993)

The Bulger murder was certainly a terrible single event, involving children killing a younger child. But what was striking was the way in which it was so easily fitted into the pre-established discourse that had given rise to moral panics. There was little attempt to put the event into proportion. Child murderers are very rare indeed. At the time of the Bulger murder there were only seven children aged between 10 and 17 detained at Her Majesty's pleasure having been convicted of murder. And five years previously, when 2-year-old Sharona Joseph was abducted in Hertfordshire by a 12-year-old and suffocated to death, because the media did not employ the moralizing discourse there was little public reaction and no suggestion that it was part of a widespread social malaise. One difference between the two cases was that the abduction of James Bulger took place in a busy shopping mall, and losing a child in such circumstances is probably every parent's nightmare. The abduction was also captured on video and given widespread publicity. A number of people who saw the children failed to do anything, thus raising questions about the decline of community and sense of responsibility for others. Finally, it was alleged that the boys had been influenced by a video nasty and this raised fears that children were being introduced to violence and immorality in new ways that escaped regulation. In sum, the circumstances of the Bulger killing were such as to trigger several anxieties and fears of a more general and diffuse nature, and the way in which the case was reported aggravated those fears. But did it amount to a moral panic?

Commentators varied in their judgement about whether the case had given rise to a moral panic. The *Guardian* editorial leader writer commented:

> A single event like the tragic murder of the Merseyside two-year old could help to give more coherence to a public debate that has remained until now improperly focused; or it could prompt a moral panic in which emotion plays a more important role than rational thinking in policy-making. Ministers still seem uncertain about which route to take, although most evidence yesterday seemed to point to their preference for the second.
>
> (The *Guardian*, 22 February 1993)

However, the Chief Rabbi Jonathan Sacks, writing a column in *The Times* some months later, seemed relieved about the media coverage and public reaction: 'That is not moral panic, but an honest recognition of the threads of collective responsibility that make society more than an aggregate of individuals' (3 December 1993). Whether the coverage in the more popular newspapers could be described as contributing to a balanced and rational debate is open to question. When the court handed down its guilty verdict, the *Daily Mail* (25 November 1993) devoted sixteen pages to the story, beginning with a front-page headline: 'Evil, Brutal and Cunning'. The *Sun* (25 November 1993) also gave it sixteen pages, with a series of shock-horror headlines: 'Driven to crime by sick sex fantasies', 'He had a blood lust and would have killed again', 'A grim warning of nightmares to come', 'Devil himself couldn't have made a better job of raising two fiends' and 'Lock them up for ever'. The last headline was quoting Members of Parliament, who were demanding that the Bulger killers should be locked up for ever; several Tory MPs were also calling for schools to bring back caning and for new laws to force parents to control children. Tucked away at the bottom of the same page was a headline, 'Exceptional case', in which the *Sun* described as 'extraordinary' a statement by Liverpool City Council saying that 'The circumstances of this case were wholly exceptional' (25 November 1993). Clearly, such a possibility did not fit in to the discourse of widespread immorality and family breakdown leading to violence, and so the paper simply dismissed it as not worthy of serious consideration, even though it may have been factually correct. The *Sun* gave more space to a story under the headline: 'It could have been my boy on the railway line', which played on the anxiety of parents imagining that it might have been their child who was abducted and murdered.

The media presentation had a lasting impact in creating a heightened sense of anxiety that could easily become a moral panic whenever elements of the discourse surrounding the Bulger case were used. Under a heading of 'Parents fear a repeat of Bulger abduction', *The Times* reported that:

> The spectre of James Bulger's abduction is still etched in the memories of British parents more than a year after he was murdered, according to a survey published today.

Out of 1,000 parents interviewed this year, 97 per cent cited the possible abduction of their children as their greatest fear. Many said that video images of the two-year-old being taken by his killers were fresh in their minds.

(*The Times*, 10 February 1994)

The stirring up of feelings of anxiety verging on panic seemed to be the aim of the *Daily Mail*'s columnist Linda Lee Potter, under the headline 'Horror as our worst fears now become sickening reality' (26 November 1993). She made extensive use of the key components of the discourse of moral decline, family breakdown and violence:

The death of James Bulger has proved a catalyst for all our worst fears. If we continue to live in a world where there is no shame in having endless children by different fathers, where marital infidelity is unimportant . . . we are doomed to live in an increasing maelstrom of horror. More children will die. There will be more young murderers. . . . We have a world where children are growing up virtually as savages. Through video shops they have recourse to scenes of evil and black magic.

(*Daily Mail*, 26 November 1993)

And, according to this discourse, there seems to be no way of escaping the risks in the nightmare scenario, except by returning to a more traditional community in which any deviance from strict moral rules is sanctioned by stigma and disgrace:

The one thing that politicians undervalue is the powerful force of public opinion. A pregnant girl got married in the Fifties because her family was disgraced if she didn't. Most married couples stayed together because it was shocking to get divorced. And the reason the majority of girls were virgins when they walked up the aisle was because it was a way to ensure their boyfriends married them.

Unmarried girls who slept around were despised and pitied as slags and whores. The feelings of the community were so powerful that it worked to a remarkable degree. As we all today

search around desperately for a solution, as we yearn to
protect our children, as we look towards the future with feelings almost akin to terror, we surely all need to try and
influence what has become unacceptable behaviour. We need
to be censorious, because God help us if we're not.

(*Daily Mail*, 26 November 1993)

Such a discourse has all the ingredients for creating a moral
panic. It asserts that immorality is rampant and we are doomed
to live in terror in a maelstrom of horror. The only solution is a
return to the past, where it is supposed that there was a close
community based on fear. Clearly, this is not a practical solution,
nor one that would be acceptable to many people; it also ignores
some real changes, such as women's greater freedom due to
economic changes and the possibility of more control over their
reproductive functions thanks to the availability of contraceptive
methods and abortion. The economic restructuring of recent years
has involved creating a flexible labour market favouring women
employees in lower-paid and often part-time jobs, which has
changed the balance of the household economy. These structural
changes are not addressed in the moralizing discourse that gives
rise to moral panics.

Politicians have been prepared to encourage and use the
moralizing discourse because it places the responsibility for
tragic events on the shoulders of others, such as single mothers
or the Church. The *Daily Mail*'s front-page headline (26
November 1993) was 'Silence in the pulpits'. It reported: 'A
bitter rift opened between Government and Church in the wake
of the James Bulger case yesterday. It began when a Minister
lambasted clergymen for failing to teach children right from
wrong. The Home Office Minister David Maclean had said, 'It is
surely part of the problem that while the Church spends its time
discussing social issues such as housing, politicians are left to
talk about the importance of right and wrong'. Not surprisingly,
the Church was furious, and the Archbishop of Canterbury's
office said he had consistently spoken out on the issue.
Politicians were not innocent when it came to picking and

choosing which bits of moral teaching to support. The Conservative Government's 'Back to Basics' moral campaign had backfired when ministers and MPs were revealed as breaking the commandment about adultery. And perhaps the problem with the media was that they did not judge the Church's traditional moral teaching on matters such as murder to be sufficiently newsworthy. The media watchdog, the Broadcasting Standards Council ordered both the BBC and ITV to apologize for their coverage of the Bulger murder case. It censured the BBC's 'Public Eye' programme for treating the case like 'suspense fiction' with the 'sensationalised' use of music and slow motion (London *Evening Standard*, 24 March 1994). Meanwhile ITV's *World in Action* was criticized for using tapes of police interviews with the accused boys, and was accused of 'violating the privacy' of 'families already riven with guilt and misery, the innocent members of which must rebuild their lives' (ibid.).

Reviewing the media coverage in the *Independent on Sunday* (28 November 1993), columnist Neal Ascherson concluded:

> Manipulation took place, of course. The television interviews with relations and policemen and teachers were all in the can weeks before the verdict, and the agenda for public concern had been drawn up. Single parents, truancy, decay of neighbourliness, poverty and crime, video nasties . . . all were studio guests in this ventriloquism game show.
>
> (The *Independent on Sunday*, 28 November 1993)

In other words, the media tend to shape their treatment of events, however rare, according to conventional formats. They also tend to develop a story line in terms of existing discourses, reflecting an assumed or already constructed public opinion, which in reality may be nothing more than a figment of the media's own imaginative capacities or worldview. The results of this treatment may not always be predictable. For example, the media people who presented the Bulger story to the public were probably themselves shocked at the passions or panics they unleashed. As Ascherson remembered:

I can still see the instant on BBC1's *Good Morning . . . with Anne and Nick show*, as James Bulger's uncle said that when the two little murderers came out of jail, 'we'll be f . . . waiting'. The two presenters froze. Anne Diamond's mouth became a black 'O' of terror. A paralysed second passed before Nick Owen began to gabble about understandable emotional stress and cut the uncle off.

(The *Independent on Sunday*, 28 November 1993)

The carefully constructed impression of a friendly 'family living room' on which a morning programme such as *Good Morning* depended was shattered by the outburst.

Although the media give space to moral campaigners and to expressions of moral outrage that may incite moral panics, they do not encourage direct action outside the law. Ascherson commented on the *Good Morning* incident:

It was memorable because it showed that a large section of our moral landscape is stage scenery; that a decent, politically liberal Star Chamber of media people and politicians still draws the limits for 'acceptable concern'. Even if we share the Star Chamber's views on crime and punishment, which I do, we have to realise that 'identifiable public opinion' has passed through its filter. The residue has been intercepted, sanitised and dumped.

(The *Independent on Sunday*, 28 November 1993)

At its best, the media's dramatization of issues may promote rational and informed debate, provided the format of discussion meets certain criteria: sufficient length for in-depth treatment, well-informed participants to put different sides of the argument, with firm but sympathetic chairing. In such circumstances, it is unlikely to give rise to a moral panic. At its worst, the media's treatment of an event or issue can be so sensationalized as to arouse fears of risk and threat that lead to disproportionate or misdirected demands for action. This was the case with the *Good Morning* outburst, which led Ascherson to comment: 'There are no "answers" in the Bulger tragedy, but even if there were, vendetta assassination would not be among them' (ibid.). A less dramatic but still significant effect of the media treatment of the Bulger case was in persuading the Home Secretary to increase the sentence on the young murderers from ten years to fifteen years. A *Panorama* television programme (9 October 1995) disclosed that the reason given by the Home Office for taking this action was that there was 'evidence of public concern'. The Home Office cited a 20,000-signature petition, which it turned out was the result of *Sun* readers sending in petition coupons from the newspaper, demanding an increase in sentence.

VIDEO NASTIES PANIC

One of the directions taken by the moral panic resulting from media representations of the Bulger murder was a revived concern about video nasties and their influence on children. Technological developments, like social and economic changes, can be viewed positively, as increasing opportunities, or negatively, as a source of increased risk. The risk element is a source of anxiety because the new technology appears to escape previous forms of regulation and its possible effects are relatively unknown, especially the effects on the vulnerable (e.g. children) or the 'marginal' groups (e.g. the 'underclass'). This was the case with the video cassette, which had a rapid take-up and spawned a whole industry of films for video and video rental shops. It was particularly attractive to poorer sections of the population as the cost of hiring a video feature film was substantially less than that of cinema seats for a couple or a family. Video films, because they were for private viewing, were regarded more leniently by the regulatory authorities, and adult content in terms of sex and violence is extremely popular. It is not surprising that they were added to the chain of signifiers in the coded discourse of 'moral decline', along with the underclass, unmarried mothers and welfare dependency.

In the Bulger trial Mr Justice Morland, sentencing the young murderers Jon Venables and Robert Thompson, said: 'I suspect exposure to violent video films may in part be an explanation for this terrible crime', on the grounds that Venables's father had rented such videos (*Sun*, 25 November 1993). This suspicion was represented as virtually proven fact by sections of the media, as witnessed by the *Sun's* headline: 'Horror Video Replay: Chilling links between James murder and tape rented by killer's dad' (ibid.). This was accompanied by a page of coloured still photographs from the video *Child's Play 3*, which the paper insisted bore an 'uncanny resemblance' to the Bulger murder. However, the transcript of the trial shows that the police officer who led the investigation disagreed, maintaining that he could find no connection between a video and the murder, and Venables's solicitor quoted the boy as saying that he had never seen it. The *Sun's* report omitted the police officer's statement and rather misleadingly concluded its story with the words: 'Merseyside Police refused to comment on the significance of the videos' (ibid.).

Next to the *Sun's* story about the video link to the murder was another headline: 'Ban Movie Nasties', quoting MPs who were calling for 'a clampdown on video movie nasties and violent TV in the wake of the Bulger trial' (ibid.). A motion from Liberal David Alton and Tory Michael Allison called for action to be taken. This brings us to the connection between moral panics and claims-makers or pressure groups, which use the heightened sense of risk to press for their predetermined objective, such as censorship legislation. David Alton, MP, was a leader of a lobby group called the Movement for Christian Democracy (MCD). This movement was able to raise £13,000 to support his campaign to attach an amendment to the Criminal Justice Bill to tighten up film and video censorship in the wake of the moral panic over the Bulger murder. It was able to employ a parliamentary draftsman to draft the amendment and it was responsible for gathering 100,000 signatures for a much-publicized petition supporting the amendment. Its newspaper, the *Christian Democrat*, boasted in June 1994 that 'with this, the MCD can be seen as coming of age politically – and can look forward to more successful campaigns' (Petley 1994: 53), and Alton was quoted as saying 'this has shown how the MCD really can affect events if it wants to, if it picks its issues, attaches them to Government bills that are going through parliament, campaigns around them' (ibid.). It saw this success as the first step in a campaign to extend censorship: 'we will now direct our campaign to the anomalies this amendment will create between what may be shown on video and what is shown on satellite, cable and terrestrial TV' (ibid.). Strangely, none of the newspapers or other media that helped to publicize the campaign against video nasties mentioned the lobby group and Alton's connection to it.

The moral campaigners made selective use of academic research. David Alton invited Professor Elizabeth Newson of Nottingham University to submit a statement, signed by herself and thirty-two fellow psychologists, psychiatrists and paediatricians, which supported his campaign. The statement was reported by the London *Evening Standard* (31 March 1994) under the heading 'U-Turn Over Video Nasties', purporting to reveal that 'Britain's top psychologists today confess that they had got it wrong in denying a link between video nasties and real life violence'. This was given widespread publicity by the popular press, although they failed to point out that the statement had been solicited by Alton and that it was far from being a U-turn as only three of the signatories had ever spoken out on the subject before. Also, it was far from being 'expert' opinion, as none of the signatories were media specialists. A few days later the Policy Studies Institute published a long-awaited report into the viewing habits of young offenders. It was funded by the main regulatory bodies, such as the Independent Television Commission, the Broadcasting Standards Council and the BBC. Its main finding was that young offenders do not have significantly different viewing habits from non-offending children of the same age. However, it did show that amongst those offenders who read newspapers, the *Sun* came out as favourite. The report was ignored by most of the popular press, including the *Sun*. The popular press also ignored a document, signed by twenty-three media academics, which questioned the whole basis of the Newson paper and stated that her conclusions went against most recent research on the media.

The escalating circulation wars between the newspapers probably had an effect on their treatment of this populist issue. Sometimes this gave rise to vicious crossfire. The *Mirror*, the *Telegraph* and the *Independent* were locked in a pricing war with the Murdoch papers, and they all joined in the attack on *Child's Play 3*, which had been shown twice by Murdoch's BSkyB satellite channel during the Bulger murder trial in November 1993 – a third screening, which would have been broadcast after the trial, was cancelled, adding to the myth that the film had played a role in the murder (Petley 1994: 53). The *Telegraph* ran a headline 'Sky drops film James's killers may have seen' (26 November 1993), and on the same day the *Mirror* did not miss the opportunity to attack its Murdoch rival in an editorial which argued that 'such violence is not only available from the local video shop. It is pumped into millions of homes virtually every night on satellite television' (26 November 1993).

In addition to the competitive media context, which inclined sections of the press to jump to the conclusion that there was a connection between videos and events like the Bulger murder, there was also a readily available moral-decline discourse which could be used to frame the issues. In the wake of another horrific murder, of 16-year-old Suzanne Capper, which also involved allegations about the influence of *Child's Play 3*, the *Mail*, noting that the police had commented on the murderers' 'ordinariness', proclaimed:

> they are the product of a society which tolerates petty crime, the break-up of families and feckless spending. It subsidises and, in many cases, encourages them. It is interesting to note that most of Suzanne's tormentors were on social security. But then those in society who are genuinely out of work but who have savings, do not receive income support. Thus are the prudent penalised while the negligent are nurtured. All this reflects a society showing reckless disregard for the survival of its own decency. An underclass is being created today which is a grave threat to Britain's future. If it is not countered, then we will continue a decline towards lawlessness and degeneracy.
>
> (*Daily Mail*, 18 December 1993)

The same discourse, linking videos, violence and an underclass, was evident at the time of the Alton amendment, when *The Sunday Times* columnist Margaret Driscoll asserted that 'the children most likely to be damaged are those being brought up in sink estates where family values no longer hold sway – the products of the 'anything goes' society' (3 April 1994). Meanwhile, in the *Mail* Lynda Lee Potter claimed that:

> there are thousands of children in this country with fathers they never see and mothers who are lazy sluts. They are allowed to do what they want, when they want. They sniff glue on building sites, scavenge for food and, until now, they were free to watch increasingly horrific videos. By 16 they are disturbed and dangerous.

> (*Daily Mail*, 13 April 1994)

Such is the nature of the many opinion columns that proliferate in the contemporary press, it was not felt necessary to draw on any research to substantiate these assertions. What was not mentioned was that a campaign in the early 1980s had already resulted in Britain having the most stringent regulatory regime over videos in the whole of western Europe, and other countries in Europe did not seem to be suffering this moral panic.

The *Daily Mail* reacted angrily to any research that threatened to dampen down the moral panic about moral decline and the collapsing family. When the Family Policy Studies Centre published a report based on a study of 2,000 families, which appeared to show that 'the family is alive and well', contrary to popular myth, although its structure was changing, the *Mail* headed its report 'The nuclear fall-out – Clash over claim that divorce can boost family' (18 November 1996).

The ideological tendency to idealize the traditional family and to equate immorality with its breakdown was severely strained by the apparent increase in the 1980s and 1990s of sexual abuse within the family. This gave rise to a sustained moral panic from 1985–6 onwards. The problem was exacerbated by the response of public authorities, which was to create agencies and units with a full-time responsibility for detecting and combating child abuse. This naturally tended to increase the number of reported cases of abuse, which further raised public consciousness of a threat. One region, Cleveland, in 1987 claimed to find evidence of widespread intrafamilial abuse and began the extensive removal of children from their families 'for their own good'. This Cleveland affair gave rise to charges and countercharges in the press about who was to blame. Two opposing stereotypical discourses emerged. In articles supporting the idea of widespread child abuse, the problem was symbolized by the incestuous father, effectively protected from retribution by the scepticism of 'patriarchal' police agencies, media and politicians, all refusing to believe children's testimony (cf. the article 'Ritual Denial', the *Guardian*, 22 March 1997). For right-wing critics, the chief folk devil was the interfering social worker, sometimes cast as a rabid left-wing feminist, determined to shatter the family unit (Jenkins 1992: 16–17). In America, an article in the conservative journal the *Weekly Standard* described the dramatic rise in sex abuse cases as 'a dangerous outbreak of mass hysteria, nurtured and abetted by a burgeoning class of therapists, shrinks and crank spiritualists with an ideological (and financial) stake in portraying children as sexual victims' (1–8 January 1996: 36). These opposing stereotypes culminated in the moral panic about satanic ritual abuse. The division of opinion was worsened by the fact that two contradictory research reports on the subject appeared in Britain in 1994. One, commissioned by the Department of Health in 1991, concluded that satanic abuse does not exist and blamed social workers and others, who put leading questions to children on the subject and then accepted their replies as proof. It did find three cases of ritual abuse (the *Independent on Sunday*, 24 April 1994). Another survey, by researchers at the University of Manchester, did not deal with satanic abuse, but claimed that ritual abuse is much more widespread than was found in the Department of Health report (*The Times*, 18 June 1994). Those who claimed to have suffered satanic abuse reacted angrily to the Department of Health Report and the favourable publicity given to it by the media.

The subjects of child sexual abuse and satanic abuse at times did threaten to become fully fledged moral panics, but on the whole the press treatment remained somewhat equivocal, the tendency to welcome sensational news being countered by ideological blinkers about the idealized family and a hostility to 'busybody' social workers. When the subject of child abuse appeared without the sensational aspects of satanism or paedophile networks the press were less inclined to generate moral indignation. A former tabloid newspaper editor, Roy Greenslade, reviewed the press's treatment of the subject of child abuse and concluded:

> Ill-treatment of children is considered inside tabloids as not merely serious and boring – like politics and news from abroad – but a turn-off. It does not add sales, and it might alienate readers.
>
> (*The Observer*, 27 October 1996)

His remarks were provoked by press treatment of a report from the National Commission of Inquiry into the Prevention of Child Abuse, sponsored by the National Society for the Prevention of Cruelty to Children. One tabloid had given it favourable publicity – the *Sun*. According to Greenslade, this exception was due to the fact that the *Sun*'s agony aunt, Deirdre Sanders, had served on the Commission, and had been invited on to it because of the many child abuse problems in her regular post bag. The *Daily Express*'s columnist and campaigner for family morals, Mary Kenny, called it 'an implausible and unreliable document, with an anti-family bias' (quoted by Greenslade, in *The Observer*, 27 October 1996). The *Mail* scornfully claimed that the report wanted to make smacking a criminal offence, although there was no such demand in the 13,000 words of the report, 'Childhood Matters'.

Greenslade drew a contrast between the tabloids' treatment of child abuse and of mugging:

> What strikes me so forcefully about the way the papers treat child abuse is the contrast with their approach to armed robbery or mugging. This kind of crime is much less prevalent

than child abuse, even if we halve the commission's figures. But lots of space is devoted to robbers and muggers.

These crimes are the subject of continuous analysis by tabloid papers. The *Daily Mail* is always urging the Home Secretary to bring in tougher sentences. Any failure to do so is seized on as a weakness of government. Feature writers and columnists are urged to enter the fray. Crusades against such crimes are a stock-in-trade of tabloid journalism and supported implicitly by the right-wing broadsheets. It is seen, as we witnessed last week, as symbolic of society's moral degeneration.

Yet papers prefer to treat every child abuse case as an isolated incident rather than as part of a trend. It is too shaming to imagine that it might be widespread. If there is something nasty in the woodshed, then leave the doors bolted. Papers would find it too intrusive and quite probably too reader-unfriendly, to make much of it.

(*The Observer*, 27 October 1996)

Although the problem of child abuse within the conventional family was something difficult for the tabloid press to accept as widespread, it had no such scruples about inflating the problem of child neglect by single mothers. In one year, 1993, there was a rapid succession of newspaper stories about 'home alone' children – in which children were said to have been left alone at home while the parent (usually a mother) had gone off on holiday. It was surely not just coincidence that this moral panic occurred in the wake of John Hughes's film *Home Alone*, which gave the media the label to attach to this form of social deviance.

The conclusion of this analysis of moral panics about the family in Britain has to be that they are the product of factors that are not unique to this country, but the way in which they have combined and been articulated here in recent decades is more likely to lead to moral panics than in other comparable societies. Of particular importance are the structure of the national press and the relative political success of a New Right ideology that has emphasized traditional moral values, encapsulated in the label 'family values'. Such has been the hegemonic triumph of this discourse that it even shaped the language of the main left-wing party, now restyled as New Labour. In order to regain a broad popular appeal after the decline of its old support base in the industrial working class, the Labour Party found itself responding to the agenda already established in the mass media by the New Right, which included moral regeneration in the form of 'family values'. By 1996 New Labour seemed to have accepted that it had no choice other than to seek to align itself with the *Daily Mail*'s moral campaigning, perhaps hoping to inflect it a little in a preferred direction, but not to challenge it.

7

FEMALE VIOLENCE AND GIRL GANGS

In several of the moral panics that we have discussed so far a common source of an increased sense of risk was that of changes in gender roles and their impact on the family, giving rise to a struggle over values and ideologies as encoded in discourses concerning what is 'natural' or essential to social order. Nowhere is this more apparent than in moral panics about female violence.

Although more attention was given to girls in the studies of club culture and Raves than was the case in the earlier studies of youth subcultures, they still appeared as relatively 'docile' and not the primary focus of moral panic. This is not the case with regard to the moral panic that began in the 1990s about increasing female violence and girl gangs. If there was one episode that crystallized the new level of concern about this issue and caused it to develop into a moral panic, it was the highly publicized attack in November 1994 on Elizabeth Hurley, the actress, model and girlfriend of Hugh Grant, star of the film *Four Weddings and a Funeral*. She was attacked in the street near her home in the Chelsea district of London by four teenage girls. The event was given extensive coverage by the mass media and prompted speculation about girl gangs and the rise of violence among young women. According to one media commentator, 'The probation service and ex-offender organizations found themselves bombarded with requests from journalists seeking out case histories to illustrate this apparent explosion of LA-style girl gang culture on the streets of Britain' (Sally Weale, in the *Guardian*, 19 September 1995).

The week after the Hurley incident, *The Sunday Times* ran a full-page feature article, complete with pictures of Elizabeth Hurley and of a girl gang wearing masks – the Busch Corner gang. Under the headline 'Sugar 'n' spice but . . . not at all nice', the article claimed that the rise of girl gangs was not confined to London, but had also been observed in Birmingham and Manchester. A youth worker was quoted as saying that 'Girl gangs have been mushrooming. They are prepared to use broken bottles, but it is the element of surprise which makes their attack successful. They target vulnerable women who don't expect to be attacked by a group of young girls' (*The Sunday Times*, 27 November 1994). It listed some of the media images of 'uncompromising and aggressive women' that had become popular and which it claimed must have influenced girls: *Tank Girl*, 'a shaven-headed, beer-swilling feminist superheroine'; *Thelma and Louise*, 'two women who turn outlaws after killing a sex attacker'; and *Nikita*, 'a glamorous but coldly efficient hitwoman' (ibid.). There then followed the obligatory reference to America as the salutory example of how bad things could become, especially in the black ghettos of Los Angeles, and where girl gangsters were featured in a magazine aimed specifically at them – *Teen Angels*.

The next step in the signification spiral was illustrated by *The Sunday Times*'s suggestion that 'Girl gangs may be just a symptom of a wider malaise produced as the taboos of female violence and vulgarity are breached in all walks of life' (27 November 1994). It quoted Home Office statistics showing that serious offences by women had risen by 250 per cent since 1973, including large increases in robberies and drugs offences. The figure of 101,000 serious crimes by women in 1993 was mentioned and said to be an increase of 12 per cent over five years, although the category of serious crimes was not defined. A victim of the Busch gang described how they started 'kicking, punching and scratching me all over' (ibid.). (The girls were reportedly fined £35 – hardly a sign of a serious violent offence.) This was followed immediately in the article by a statement that on estates in Britain's inner cities police had observed gangs of young girls, 'some armed with machetes and army knives, competing with men for a share of the drugs trade' (ibid.). The article seemed to have a very elastic notion of serious crime and violence, seemingly equating kicking and scratching with the use of machetes and army knives.

A further element in escalating the panic was the extension of the source and location of the risk beyond working-class girls from the ghettos to violent middle-class women in respectable venues. Even 'thirty-something professionals' at a 'media party in central London' were said to have 'smashed wine glasses, [thrown] punches and hurled obscenities' (ibid.). Meanwhile:

> Behind the closed doors of British married life, a similar pattern is emerging. The first national helpline for male victims has been set up and has been swamped with calls from battered husbands. Victims include those from unexpected walks of life: soldiers, policemen and rugby players.
>
> (*The Sunday Times*, 27 November 1994)

More evidence of the mounting risk of female violence was presented to the media by a 1995 report, 'Freedom's children: work, relationships and politics for 18–34-year-olds in Britain today', commissioned by the think-tank Demos from the British Household Panel Study and the MORI survey organization. The report commented that 'Young women are exhibiting what have typically been seen as male attributes – they are less emotional than older women, more willing to take risks and seek excitement in such things as foreign travel, parachuting, rock climbing and drug taking' (quoted in the *Guardian*, 19 September 1995). The researchers also compiled a rather novel 'pleasure in violence index', where they constructed a series of questions to assess people's attitudes to violence. It seemed to suggest that girls aged 15 to 17 were 'taking more pleasure in violence' (ibid.) and were more likely to resort to it than their male contemporaries.

However, some experts were sceptical about these claims of a rising tide of female violence. A senior probation officer at the Inner London Probation Service Women's Centre was quoted as saying: 'One woman does something somewhere and immediately there's a great moral panic. People think there's an epidemic of it' (quoted in the *Guardian*, 19 September 1995). Statistics and research produced in August 1995 by the National Association of Probation Officers did show an increase in the number of women jailed for offences involving violence, but according to the Assistant General Secretary of the association, who carried out some of the research interviews of women in prison:

> The image of amoral female gangs is wide of the mark. There has been a rise of 50 per cent in the number of women jailed for violence in the last three years, but the reasons are complex. The majority of the group are characterised by neglect, personal abuse, drug or alcohol abuse and low self-esteem. Many have themselves been the victim of violence.
>
> (*Guardian*, 19 September 1995)

Criminologists also put the statistics in perspective. To begin with, women made up less than 4 per cent of the total prison population. Figures for 31 August 1995 put the total female prison population at 1,984, compared with 51,362 men.

In 1996 the moral panic about young violent females gathered pace again as a result of two more highly publicized incidents. In April, in Corby, 13-year-old Louise Allen died after intervening to stop a fight. Two other 13-year-old girls were accused of causing her death by kicking her. Her headmaster, in expressing his grief, sought to maintain a sense of proportion by saying, 'I don't think there is a culture of violence. Nobody set out on Monday night to kill anybody.' This did not deter the *Sun*, which had the front page headline 'Kicked to death by 30 schoolgirl yobs'. The *Sunday Express* (5 May 1996) followed with a feature article that mixed fact and fiction, with the headline 'Girlz N the Hood: After a schoolgirl is kicked to death, female gangs bring new fear'. It featured interviews with members of the Downtown Girls gang of Romford, Essex, whose behaviour was described as 'reminiscent of scenes from the American cult movie, "Boyz N The Hood" ', and a statement that research for the *Sunday Express* by a forensic psychologist revealed that 'by the year 2013, perpetrators of assaults are as likely to be female as male'. Blending this rather dubious statistical projection with references to popular entertainment, it quoted the author of the screenplay of a forthcoming feature film on girl gangs, who stated:

> A new breed of violent and armed girl gangs is emerging on the streets of the UK and carrying out horrific attacks, usually on the most vulnerable targets. Girls of 13 and upwards go out in packs to mug and maim, using knives, bottles and screwdrivers. They can fight like boys and have a craving for violence.
>
> (*Sunday Express*, 5 May 1996)

The *Sunday Express* story was accompanied by photographs of Louise Allen and of two black girls with the caption 'The menacing new face of fear in Britain as teenage girls wait on a city estate to pounce on a fresh robbery victim' (ibid.). There was also a picture of the female star of the film *Trainspotting*, about heroin-taking in Edinburgh, who 'may appear in a new movie about violence among young girls' (ibid.), and a graph showing an increase of violent attacks by women between 1987 and 1994.

The two girls responsible for the death of Louise Allen were eventually brought to trial for manslaughter, and most of the press made it a front-page story. The discourse had all the elements required to generate a moral panic: suggestions of a spreading risk from out-of-control folk devils – in this case, teenage girls acting against their feminine nature and behaving like men. The *Daily Mail*'s heading was 'How Girls Aged 13 Became Killers: A father serving life in jail for murder, a culture of street gang violence' (15 November 1996). Both girls had fathers who had convictions for violence and the girls were described as being members of the Canada Street gang, 'a group of up to 20 young girls who were allowed to spend their evenings

hanging around the area from which they took their name'
(ibid.). This hardly amounted to evidence of an organized gang
and could have been applied as a description to almost any group
of working-class children in the past who spent their time
hanging around the street and occasionally causing trouble. In
keeping with the required format of the discourse, we are
presented with a stark contrast between the evil and unnatural
character of the gang girls and the good, typically female quali-
ties of the victim. The accused girls were described as having 'sat
impassively' through the trial (a similar comment was made
about the young killers of James Bulger) and the leader was said
to have 'just turned evil in a group' (ibid.). Meanwhile, the tragic
victim, Louise, was described in a separate profile article as
having been brought up to 'be polite, respect your elders and
have good manners', keeping up 'a tradition of service in the
church, assisting younger children with their reading' and acting
'like a mother figure to many of the younger children' (ibid.).

Some liberal press commentators sought to stem the rising
moral panic. Libby Purves wrote in *The Times* (19 November
1996):

> Are schoolgirls getting rougher? Discuss, writing your answer
> on one side only, and refrain from setting fire to the pigtails of
> the girl in front. We may as well think about it, since it is plain
> that the next moral panic to overwhelm us . . . is going to be
> about wild girls.
>
> It has already begun. We have been favoured with moodily
> scrambled TV profiles of the girls who mugged Liz Hurley; we
> have been informed by *Panorama*, from abstruse calculations,
> that 'by the year 2016' women will be as violent as men. More
> seriously and incontrovertibly, we have been shaken by the
> case of the two 13-year-old girls who killed Louise Allen in a
> street fight in Corby, and who now plead guilty to
> manslaughter.
>
> (*The Times*, 19 November 1996)

She presented the feminist and anti-feminist explanations for the
apparent increase in female violence. The feminist analysis said

that girls were once educated to be more physically restrained, weak and dependent, sometimes deliberately maimed (Chinese women had bound feet, western women wore corsets). This led to girls internalizing their aggression and ending up prone to self-harm and mental illness. All this was now changing with women's liberation and co-education, and there was bound to be an increase in women's sexual predatoriness and capacity for physical aggression. This was reflected in films and fashion. The anti-feminist analysis pursued a similar line, but drew on the old fear of 'harridans and harpies to regard the change as morally and physically disastrous, an outrage against nature which will bring down civilisation' (ibid.). Purves's liberal conclusion was that the problem was not one of gender, but of young people without job prospects who find comfort in belonging to a pack.

The feminist argument was put by Lucy Johnston in *The Observer* (17 November 1996); she claimed that there was a myth going around TV studios, newspaper offices and academic institutions to the effect that there was not as much violent and sexual abuse of women as early feminism believed, and that the perpetrators of violence are increasingly likely to be women. Reviewing the evidence put forward by the recent *Panorama* TV programme, she insisted there were no reputable statistics to back up their MORI poll finding that women were more likely to beat up their male partners than vice versa. A 1994 survey by New Scotland Yard in London found 9,800 women were battered by their partners, against 887 battered men. And although the much publicized hostels for battered men had had six national launches, all closed within three months and no one had ever slept in one of their beds. And whilst *Panorama* used Home Office statistics to show that violent crimes had increased from 10 to 16 per cent of reported crime since 1987, the Home Office admitted that a violent crime could even include a 'deliberate push leading to a skin abrasion' (quoted by Johnston in *The Observer*, 17 November 1996). Furthermore, estimates based on percentage increases were often misleading because of the tiny numbers involved. For example, a breakdown of the 1994 Home Office figures on those sentenced to prison was as follows: murder

– women 8, men 182; sexual offences and rape – women 9, men 1,920; violent woundings – women 107, men 1,174.

The backlash against early feminism is explained by Johnston as in part brought on by organizations attempting to redress the balance against men, such as the False Memory Society, which discounts claims of memories of childhood sexual abuse, and Familes Need Fathers, which campaigns on behalf of men whose wives and children have fled. Ironically, she admits, some of the anti-feminist ideas have been given legitimacy by feminists themselves, who concede to the backlash, claiming that 1970s feminism is dead. She cites Alex Kirsta's book *Deadlier Than the Male*, which claimed that women's natural aggression is suppressed by a society that forces them to be caring and kind, and Camille Paglia's *Vamps and Tramps*, which argues that battered women are not victims but goddesses of men's fear. The reason why the new generation of feminists is co-opting the backlash, according to Johnston, is that they were influenced by the experience of 1980s consumerism, and 'they want to assert that women make choices about their lives, including whether to live in abusive and violent relationships' (*The Observer*, 17 November 1996). In America, new feminists have coined the term 'women with agency', and 'agency' means power, control and choice. Women with agency are the opposite of victims.

Whether or not feminism is a major cause of the moral panic about women and violence is a difficult question to answer. However, it is a question sometimes raised by the media. The London *Evening Standard* opened an article on 'Danger women: Women are becoming more violent, and according to a new survey, television is to blame' by stating:

> In a new survey, positive role models, or more precisely, positively awful role models in Seventies TV series, such as *Charlie's Angels*, combined with feminist influences, are blamed for 'a new generation of aggressive women'.
>
> (*Evening Standard*, 1 February 1996)

According to research by the University of Michigan, which followed more than 200 girls from childhood in the late 1970s until their mid-twenties, television series such as *Charlie's Angels* and *The Bionic Woman* represented a 'feminist breakthrough'. Through these images of violent heroines, the researcher L. Rowell Huesman maintained, 'Girls get desensitised to violence, just like boys. When heroines' aggressive acts are portrayed positively, girls conclude it is a good way to solve problems' (*Evening Standard*, 1 February 1996). Although there may be a case for media images having an effect on behaviour, other research suggests it is not a direct effect and it depends on the conjunction of a number of other factors, which may need to be investigated in each case of female violence. As one reviewer put it:

> At the same time, young girls were also watching series in the style, for instance, of The Flying Nun and Bewitched (about a domesticated witch with a wriggly nose). Since neither have resulted in a sudden increase in the convent population or a rush to the occult, one might suggest (backed by many academic studies) that the direct link between television and violence is, at best, unproven. And that escapism does not automatically lead to emulation.
>
> (*Evening Standard*, 1 February 1996)

As Alix Kirsta writes in *Deadlier Than the Male*, women's violence, like men's, is nurtured by a diversity of complex environmental and psychological factors, and they may commit violence for numerous reasons, including poverty, boredom, isolation, fear, greed, kicks, desire for attention, power and dominance, or in self-defence. The reason for the moral panic may be that feminism has called into question the popular discourse according to which women are allegedly biologically determined to be 'natural' carers, nurturers, too 'nice' to do harm, and in which women who commit a violent crime must be outside the normal – 'bad or mad'. Although the discourse which divides women into either 'earth mother and angels' or 'mad and bad' may still appear in media accounts of female violence, it is contradicted by feminist discourse and by more recent popular cultural images in films such as *Thelma and Louise, Single White*

Female and *Blue Steel*, and other portrayals of women hitting back. These media portrayals may not cause women to act more violently, but they do call into question the traditional discourse in which it was taken for granted that such behaviour was unnatural and so deviant. In that respect it may create a greater sense of risk, which can lead to a backlash and moral panics.

8

MORAL PANICS ABOUT SEX ON THE SCREEN

Social and moral order is periodically imagined to be at risk due to technological and cultural developments that produce representations of sexuality which break previously accepted norms about what is publicly acceptable. Moral panics about sexual images on the screen (film, television and the Internet) have increased, not simply because of the increase in channels of communication – increased television channels, cable, satellite and the Internet – but also because this increase has provided the press with an ever-expanding source of 'news'. The press have welcomed the kind of controversy about popular culture which is generated by moral entrepreneurs and pressure groups claiming that popular films or programmes might have dangerous social effects, especially on children, young people and the family. In this chapter we will focus on the role of pressure groups and moral campaigners in relation to moral panics concerning representations of sexuality on the screen. In contrast to our review of the mugging moral panic, which concentrated on decoding media texts, the focus here might seem to have more in common with American studies of moral panics as *collective-behaviour* or *group* phenomena. However, we will also examine the ways in which the media themselves discursively construct what appears to be a moral panic, even if it is difficult to measure how widespread or deeply felt the panic is among the population.

As was suggested in Chapter 1, recent American sociological accounts have been particularly inclined to view moral panics as episodes of group behaviour, rather than primarily a media phenomenon which may or may not affect behaviour and lead to social actions, such as legislation or other action by relevant authorities. Such studies have tended to adopt a social-psychological perspective, viewing moral panics in terms of concepts about collective behaviour, deviant behaviour, leadership and social movements. For example, Erich Goode and Nachman Ben-Yehuda reject accounts, such as that of Stuart Hall *et al.* (1978) regarding the mugging moral panic, which they describe as being based on 'the assumption that elites dominate social institutions to the extent that they can control or dictate human consciousness and behaviour' (Goode and Ben-Yehuda 1994: 3). Hall and his colleagues did attempt to analyse the process by which certain ideological assumptions shaped news stories in the particular historical context of Britain in the 1970s, which produced a signification spiral and amplification of an alleged social threat; but it was certainly not presented as a scientific generalization about elites dictating human consciousness and behaviour. By contrast, Goode and Ben-Yehuda's approach is couched in terms of scientific generalization, viewing moral panics as 'episodes of collective action' which 'can be regarded as a test for theories of human behaviour in general' (ibid.: 4) They also emphasize measurement as a scientific element in their approach and focus on group behaviour:

> In these episodes, people have become intensely concerned about a particular issue or perceived threat – which, *as measured by concrete indicators*, turns out not to be especially damaging – and have *assembled, and taken action*, to remedy the problem; yet somehow, at a later point in time, they lost interest in the issue or threat, often turning their attention to other matters.
>
> (Goode and Ben-Yehuda 1994: 4; italics mine)

Without necessarily accepting all their criteria for defining a moral panic, involving measurement of disproportionality and the need for a group to have assembled and taken action, it is possible to say that the approach of Goode and Ben-Yehuda is useful for studying the relationship between a succession of moral panics and a moral campaign linked to a social movement. This is the case with respect to the anti-permissiveness movement in Britain since the 1960s and its moral campaigns against representations of sexuality on the screen, especially the role of the National Viewers' and Listeners' Association, led by Mrs Mary Whitehouse. It is a case in which moral panics can be seen to have taken place when, as Goode and Ben-Yehuda put it, four territories overlap – *deviance*, *social problems*, *collective behaviour* and *social movements*:

> The territory occupied by deviance accounts for the *moral* part of the moral panic: behaviour regarded as immoral is more likely to generate public concern and fear than is more traditional, conventional behaviour. The territory that is occupied by social problems accounts for the *public concern* part of the moral panic: when much of the public is aware of and concerned about a given condition, regardless of its objective status, sociologically, it must be regarded as a social problem – and certainly the panic represents an extremely heightened form of awareness and concern. The territory occupied by collective behaviour accounts for the *volatility* of moral panics: the fact that, much like fads, they erupt suddenly and usually unexpectedly, and, in like manner, fairly swiftly subside and disappear – or lose their fervid quality in the process of becoming institutionalized. The territory occupied by social movements addresses the issue of the *organization* and *mobilization* of concerned segments of the population to address and change specific social conditions.
>
> (Goode and Ben-Yehuda 1994: 52–3)

The first moral panic about representations of sexuality on television was partly brought on by the rapidity with which the distribution of television sets in Britain came about, rising from

0.2 per cent of homes in 1947 to 39.8 in 1955 and then 90.8 in 1964. It was at this point that sections of the population adhering to 'respectable' values suddenly found the legitimacy of those values and their lifestyle challenged in their own homes, producing a sense of increasing risk. Mrs Mary Whitehouse, a housewife and teacher who had been involved in the Moral Rearmament movement (MRA), recounts in her autobiography how she was appalled to find that the schoolchildren she was taking for 'sex education' were watching television every evening and taking from it values that were completely opposed to her traditional Christian moral values. The 'Clean-Up TV' campaign (CUTV) was officially launched on 27 January 1964 by Mary Whitehouse and her friend Norah Buckland, the wife of a clergyman and another MRA supporter. Their local paper, the *Birmingham Evening Mail*, carried the headline 'Mothers Will Campaign for High TV Morals' (23 January 1964). This was quickly followed by other press coverage of their manifesto and the planned meeting at Birmingham Town Hall on 5 May 1964. Headlines included 'Wives Rap BBC over TV Smut' and 'Two Women Fight "Disbelief and Dirt" on TV'. As two media sociologists, Michael Tracey and David Morrison, commented:

> Captivated by the news potential of two middle-aged, middle-class women campaigning against sex and the powerful BBC, the press provided the necessary impetus for the campaign. By August the same year Whitehouse was to be claiming a Manifesto with 235,000 signatures and 7000 letters of support.
>
> (Tracey and Morrison 1979: 43)

An estimated 2,000 people attended the launch meeting of CUTV, which in 1965 became the National Viewers' and Listeners' Association (NVALA). In a position paper in January 1964, Whitehouse stated the new movement's concern: 'Men and women and children listen and view at risk of serious damage to their morals, their patriotism, their discipline and their family' (quoted in Tracey and Morrison 1979: 44). Within this discursive formation of morals, patriotism, discipline and family, it is sexual

'permissiveness' and the explicitness of sexual behaviour represented on television which generated the severest criticism. Other
studies of anti-pornography crusades have suggested that sexually
exciting material provides a 'summary symbol for threats and
challenges to the life-style of anti-pornography crusaders'
(Zurcher *et al.* 1973: 70). Peter Cominos, in his analysis of the
relationship between Victorian sexual respectability and the
prevailing social and economic system, described the way in
which sexual respectability – continence before marriage, late
marriage and restraint thereafter – was seen as intimately related
to the desire to maintain and improve both economic circumstances and social position (Cominos 1963: 223; discussed in
Wallis 1976). The widening availability of contraceptive technology in the postwar era broke the link which buttressed a
repressive Victorian morality by ending the almost inevitable
correlation between sexual indulgence and social and economic
ruin. This had a particularly strong impact on the precariously
balanced lower middle class from which Mrs Whitehouse and
many of her supporters came. Sexual permissiveness thus represented one of the most fundamental challenges of new norms and
values to traditional respectability, undermining a central and
highly emotionally charged component.

In its early years the NVALA, or National VALA ('valour') as
its prefers to be known, shared the conspiracy beliefs of Moral
Rearmament (MRA) that the Christian values of the nation were
being threatened by the forces of world communism and a 'fifth
column' within, for whom moral change and the transformation
of sexual behaviour were a means of undermining capitalist
society as a whole (cf. the NVALA journal, *Viewer and Listener*,
autumn 1970: 3; spring 1971: 4). NVALA members accused one
Director-General of the BBC of 'encouraging and harbouring
near-communists on his staff' (Whitehouse 1972: 88). The *Sun*
published an article on 3 December 1965 under the headline
'Moral Rearmament and the Clean-Up TV Campaign', which
asked: 'Who is behind the efficiently run and publicity conscious
campaign to clean-up British television? Is it Moral Rearmament,
the wealthy international, semi-religious organization?' Mrs

Whitehouse denied that the two movements were linked, although she agreed that she had learned a great deal from MRA, and they certainly shared the same objective of rechristianizing the culture and combating 'alien' or deviant influences. In November 1967 Whitehouse wrote an 'Open Letter to the Prime Minister', in which she expressed a concern with 'the part played by broadcasting, and television in particular, at this point in our history when Britain is in the process of taking on a character alien to herself' (*National Viewers and Listeners Association News*, no. 2, November 1967).

Children were seen as particularly vulnerable to new styles of life and modes of thought, belief and behaviour displayed on television. 'Children . . . are pressurised into alien patterns of behaviour . . . ' (Whitehouse 1972: 134). The protection of the child was used to legitimate the urgency and stridency of the NVALA's message, which would have been less easily supported by a demand for the reinstatement of the values of just one section of the population. Although the NVALA claimed to speak for the 'moral and religious values of the mass of the people' (Whitehouse 1967: 119), this rhetoric was sometimes contradicted by their occasional presentation of themselves as a beleaguered minority in an increasingly alien culture.

The NVALA from the start had all the characteristics of a moral crusade, which persists in its discourse even thirty years after its inception, giving rise to periodic episodes of moral panic. Its discourse is constructed in terms of a fight between the forces of good and those of evil (the folk devils are often an elite of intellectuals, such as television producers and writers). The debate is said to be concerned with 'genuine freedom' or 'total licence'; 'cultural responsibility' or 'cultural anarchy' (Whitehouse 1972: 122). NVALA members 'defend decency', while their opponents' views contain 'the essence of the worst kind of dictatorship' (ibid.). NVALA seeks to defend 'accepted standards' or 'sound standards' (Whitehouse 1967: 34, 54), while its opponents seek to use television 'for purposes alien to the character of the nation and the true interest of the British people' (ibid.: 171), with the result that they become 'pliant material for any kind of alien philosophy' (ibid.: 165). There is still a rudimentary apocalyptic vision in NVALA ideology signified by the idea that 'things are getting worse'. This remains as strong as ever, as indicated by Norris McWhirter's speech to the NVALA annual conference in 1994:

> When one hears people talking of Mary and VALA they say 'Oh, we can't stand censorship'. Could I just suggest to you that what some programmes trade in is, in fact, itself censorship – censorship of decency! I can give you a motto which would be helpful in the present situation: 'Cheer up – things are getting worse!' and I say that advisedly because it is only when things are appalling that the body politic will begin to move.
>
> (*The Viewer and Listener*, summer 1994)

Although the original protest soon took institutionalized form and built up an effective lobbying organization, its membership remained fairly small. It grew to some 165,000 members (according to Stuart Wavell in *The Sunday Times*, 5 December 1993). These members also monitored broadcasts on radio and television and were asked to complete cards to indicate whether programmes infringed the standards which they were pledged to uphold. They were also urged to contact broadcasting authorities and voice their complaints. Its most effective tactic was public statements to the press by its highly articulate leader, Mrs Whitehouse, until she retired in 1994. It has also organized petitions to Parliament. The second petition in the 1970s, which was organized in association with the Christian moral crusade, the 'Festival of Light', obtained some 1,350,000 signatures. On her retirement, Mrs Whitehouse could claim that her efforts had led to the establishment of the Broadcasting Standards Council, which monitors television on matters of morals, taste and decency, and had also led to broadcasting being brought within the remit of the Obscene Publications Act.

Perhaps what this moral crusade was most successful in achieving was the establishment of a discourse which could be called upon and tapped into whenever a new development presented an opportunity for moral entrepreneurs to create a renewed panic about a threat to morals. For example, when two children murdered the 2-year-old James Bulger the *Sunday Telegraph* ran a two-page feature article with the headline 'Mary's fears come home to roost', which began:

> One blurred photograph from a shopping centre video has become the picture of the decade: the image that made the nation reel in self-loathing and horror. Not since the Moors murder, which made Myra Hindley and Ian Brady the most execrated pair in Britain, has there been a crime to make the nation's heart contract like this. But this time there was a new element of horror. A trusting child being led away by another child: the double death of innocence. In the week that has followed, outrage has been supplanted by collective guilt and the questions: what have we done? And left undone? ... A generation ago, those who feared that out-of-control liberalism was destroying society, voiced their fears. They were led by Mary Whitehouse, who became the symbol of all things that enlightened liberals despised. Last week even they began to wonder whether we should have paid more attention to her warnings. Her fears were centred on the increasingly powerful effect of television.
>
> (The *Sunday Telegraph*, 21 February 1993)

Mrs Whitehouse was quick to seize on technological and social developments that could be seen as a source of new moral threat – homes with multiple television sets and videos. She was quoted in the article as saying: 'Seven out of ten children have TV sets in their own bedrooms and since the advent of videos, there can be no such thing as a nine o'clock watershed, no way children can be protected' (ibid.).

The *Sunday Telegraph*'s correspondent drew a fearful conclusion from Mary Whitehouse's diagnosis, indicative of the moral panic:

> The unthinkable sub-text to the murder of little James Bulger is, of course, the concern that we have created a generation of anti-social young people who have grown up with a television set as their best friend and constant companion, with video

nasties, violence and sensational sex as the stuff of everyday life, in a world which offers little explicit moral guidance.

(The *Sunday Telegraph*, 21 February 1993)

There could be no greater tribute to the success of this moral entrepreneur and her movement in establishing the discourse of moral threat that could be called upon to 'make sense' of each new source of concern. As one specialist in media policy said on her retirement, she succeeded in linking together sex and violence:

She was always known as the sex and violence campaigner and I have never, never been able to understand how it is that a campaigning organization got away with linking a series of images or acts in which people do harm to each other and a series of images or acts in which people give pleasure to each other. From the very beginning she succeeded in linking them together as if they were of equal evil and that is what I find most objectionable.

(Steve Barnett, quoted in *The Independent on Sunday*, 22 May 1994)

The consumption of visually erotic material can usually be construed as a 'victimless transaction' (Duster 1970), since the consumer is normally thought of as being a willing party. However, the discourse of the NVALA transformed the presentation of erotic stimulating material into a circumstance in which there is a victim, by protesting against the public visibility of the sexual material, designating the young as vulnerable and liable to corruption by it, and presenting themselves as the defenders of children and of the unwitting viewer in the sanctity and privacy of their home (Wallis 1976: 293). The BBC, which was regarded as a former bastion of the traditional religious values of the 'respectable' classes, became a particular target for such protest as it came increasingly to reflect the norms and values of contemporary consumption-oriented society, and was seen to have deserted its traditional constituency and so dramatically brought home the loss of status of respectable morality and its bearers.

The questions still remaining to be answered are: why was sex the main focus of protest and why especially its representations on television? The first answer can be found in the observation of those who have interviewed and studied Mary Whitehouse and her movement concerning their thinking regarding secularization:

> To 'remove the myth of God from the minds of man is the priority of the atheistic humanist and communist'. Thus in her mind the question of sex is inextricably linked to the process of secularisation within our culture It is the inversion of a theocratic society into *demos*, or, in her eyes, the demotic society. She notes: 'Those whom the Gods wish to destroy they first make mad' and so the seeds of lunacy are scattered by the iconoclasts – that man is sufficient unto himself, that happiness is gratification, that sex and love are the same thing.' To abandon religion is to embark on the not so slow slide into moral chaos.
>
> (Tracey and Morrison 1979: 184)

For these moral crusaders, sexual attitudes and representations were a prominent part of the repertoire of those who wished to radically change the existing social order. The churches and the BBC were failing in their duty to uphold sacred values, and their acquiescence to increasing 'permissiveness' and moral relativism left the field open to those who wished to bring about those radical changes.

The answer to the second question, 'why television?', is that television breached the defensive wall between the public and private spheres and beamed its profane images into the sanctuary of the home. From the 1960s, British television, compared with its counterparts in America, gave more scope to dramatists, satirists and producers to experiment and test the boundaries of accepted conventions of 'morals, taste and decency'. America had a much larger and more vociferous religious constituency and its television remained relatively bland and did not give rise to moral panics to the same degree (criticism tended to be directed at Hollywood films). A typical example was the series *The Wednesday Play*, which the BBC started in 1964 and which Mrs Whitehouse and her members viewed as the quintessence of 'kitchen sink drama', reflecting some of the violence of language and manifest sexuality of inner city life. On 5 November 1970 the BBC broadcast a play by Dennis Potter called 'Angels are so Few', which led to complaints from Whitehouse and other members of the NVALA. One woman who wrote to complain about what she referred to as this 'disgusting' play received a response from the BBC's Secretariat which contained the following comments:

> We accept that the play was very outspoken and forthright and unusually harsh in its text and imagery. If we had transmitted it solely to shock or to excite by its salacity, then indeed we would be very culpable. I hope, however, that you may believe we had better reasons for transmitting it than those.... I wonder if some of the unease which you and some others feel at the present time arises from the fact that sex is a subject on which there has been such a marked change in public attitudes and tastes in recent years. Whether we like it or not, subjects which were once regarded as taboo are now discussed openly in the presence of members of both sexes and the range of topics thought of as private has shrunk dramatically. It is inevitable that this shift in acceptability should be reflected to some extent in our programmes.
>
> (quoted in Tracey and Morrison 1979: 99–100; the letter is in the NVALA archives)

The NVALA member was not in the least satisfied with this claim to be simply reflecting a changed 'reality' and wrote in her reply:

> Sex is still the same as it always was, the only thing is that it is being treated differently. 'Familiarity breeds contempt' is an old saying, and sex is not a thing to be treated contemptibly; it should not be treated lightly or casually. I agree with you, 'things which were taboo are now discussed openly' and how much better is the world for that – very, very much worse, and the topics previously dealt with privately would do well to remain private.
>
> (quoted in Tracey and Morrison 1979: 99–100; the letter is in the NVALA archives)

The same sense of moral outrage, sometimes reaching panic proportions, at the use of public broadcasting channels to transmit representations of sexuality into the private sphere of the home, has continued to produce complaints from the NVALA to the broadcasting authorities. They have frequently been given headline treatment by the press, especially when they concerned new or popular programmes. After the BBC plays, the spotlight turned on to the new soap operas which attracted some of the largest peak-time television audiences. The BBC launched its most popular soap opera, *EastEnders*, in 1985 in an attempt to raise its falling viewing figures, which were suffering under the competitive pressures from the more popular programmes of independent television. In contrast to imported soap operas from America, such as *Dynasty* and *Dallas*, which showed the glamorous lifestyles of the rich, the British soap opera had a commitment to reflect the realities of contemporary inner city life. As the producer of *EastEnders*, Julia Smith, explained:

> We decided to go for a realistic, fairly outspoken type of drama which could encompass stories about homosexuals, rape, unemployment, racial prejudice, etc. in a believable context. Above all we wanted realism. Unemployment, exams, racism, birth, death, dogs, babies, unmarried mums – we didn't want to fudge any issue except politics and swearing.
>
> (Julia Smith, quoted in Buckingham 1987: 16)

Mrs Whitehouse and the NVALA attacked it from the start and their complaints were given extensive coverage and amplification by the press. As David Buckingham, in his book *Public Secrets: EastEnders and its Audience*, points out:

> Of course, Mary Whitehouse makes for good copy, and for more 'sexy' headlines; and indeed, in certain instances, journalists appear to make direct challenges to her to respond. Intriguingly, the *Evening Standard* carried a report on the day before the programme came on the air (18 February 1985) which suggested that Whitehouse had already made complaints about EastEnders being 'too violent'. At least in

this case, it would seem that she was 'set up' by the popular press in order to generate controversy.

(Buckingham 1987: 135)

There are many examples of the way in which politicians along with 'the popular press and the Whitehouse lobby feed off each other' (ibid.). In 1987 it seemed as if Mary Whitehouse's attacks on soap opera episodes were a constant feature in the tabloid press. At the annual conference of the NVALA she was joined on the platform by Conservative MP Gerald Howarth, to whom she pledged backing for his Anti-Obscenity Bill, and she gave a warning of the perils of *EastEnders*: 'It is at our peril and our children that we allow this series with its verbal aggression and atmosphere of physical violence, its homosexuals, blackmailing pimp and prostitute, lies, deceit and bad language to go unchallenged' (*Daily News*, 4 April 1987). She received widespread publicity and claimed that *EastEnders* was having to clean up its act as a result. However, the Howarth Bill failed and she was soon criticizing *EastEnders* for its 'chronic excesses', which she said were unscrupulously manipulating the minds and hearts of children in a battle for viewing figures. In July 1988 she protested vehemently about an episode which showed the rape ordeal of the character Kathy Beale. The press published her demand for a public apology from the Chairman of the BBC governors, and it was interpreted as a victory when the BBC issued a warning about the explicit content before showing the weekend omnibus edition. She now felt she was having success in influencing the political climate. *The Daily Telegraph* announced 'Clean-up threat to television by Thatcher' (9 June 1988), disclosing that the Prime Minister was turning her attention to the media as part of her third term campaign to improve the 'moral health' of society. In 1989 an episode of *EastEnders* showing a gay couple kissing on the lips brought a concerted expression of outrage from the NVALA and Conservative MPs, supported by sections of the press who described the episode in detail.

Frequently, in their fascination with soap opera 'scandals' it seemed that, like the soap opera, the press reports were concerned with exploring moral issues and with testing the limits of morally acceptable behaviour. Both were preoccupied with investigating deviance of various kinds, particularly involving sex and violence:

> The press had an interest in reporting the NVALA's complaints and amplifying them, even if they threatened to excite a moral panic. But at the same time the stories possessed an uneasy combination of voyeuristic fascination and moral condemnation: they brought areas of private experience into the public eye, allowing readers a vicarious glimpse of 'forbidden' behaviour, yet they also enabled them to maintain a safe distance from which they could pass moral judgement.
>
> (Buckingham 1987: 140)

In this sense it may be that readers and viewers colluded with the press in allowing themselves to be shocked, and they may even have gone along with a 'simulated' moral panic. But to what extent they were really experiencing moral panic on the basis of what they had viewed rather than what they had read about programmes or films it is hard to judge.

Many complaints letters received by the broadcasting authorities about allegedly 'shocking' films on television did seem to come from people who had read a newspaper article about the film rather than seen it themselves. This was the case, for example, with respect to many of the complaints letters about the film *The Last Temptation of Christ*, shown on Channel 4 on 6 June 1995, which included a dream sequence in which Christ made love to Mary Magdalene. Channel 4 received nearly 6,000 complaints and the Independent Television Commission, 1,400. However, analysis of the letters, many of which had multiple signatures, shows that a large number of the signatories had not themselves seen the film, and some of the letters had been elicited by pressure groups. The 'watchdog' specifically set up by Mrs Thatcher to regulate the moral content of television, the Broadcasting Standards Council, received twelve letters complaining about the film in the period June–July 1995, one of which included 906 signatures, another forty-two signatures, and a third written on behalf of forty-two churches with a membership of 2,500 (the analysis of this case was carried out as part of my ESRC research project on 'Moral Regulation and Television'). The moral campaigners were also beginning to express a feeling of disillusionment with the effect of letter-writing and dismay at the toothlessness of regulatory bodies, and were advocating boycotting the goods of companies whose advertisements were shown during the screening of the offending film. As John Beyer, General Secretary of NVALA, explained: 'In our experience, the broadcasting establishment is impervious to criticism. Advertisements sustain commercial broadcasters and are therefore a legitimate target if the broadcasters will not respond to complaints in a meaningful way' (*The Observer*, 18 June 1995). The tactic met with some success, as Channel 4 was forced to apologize to Tesco and the relief agency World Vision for placing their advertisements next to *The Last Temptation of Christ*.

Mrs Whitehouse had retired from the fray, although she still made public statements, but her work had been successful in the eyes of many. She herself was regarded with more respect than ever before, and her moral campaign had become a self-sustaining feature in some newspapers, such as the *Daily Mail*. As the liberal *Guardian* noted, in an article discussing the *Daily Mail*'s moral campaign about sex on television, particularly against Channel 4:

> During the 1980s the sole complainant in virtually every case was Mary Whitehouse and her National Viewers and Listeners Association. Compliant rent-a-quote Tory MPs came to her aid, forming the backbone to stories with headlines which begin: 'Storm over . . . ' or 'Fury over . . . ' or 'Protest at . . . '. Jeremy Isaacs, as excoriated in his day as C4's chief executive as Michael Grade is today, referred to all such stories as 'Storm overs'. In the last five years, having created a climate in which C4 is synonymous with sin, the Mail doesn't need to rely on outsiders to foment 'storms'. It is now assumed that readers will only need to hear about another 'shocking' programme. Everyone among the Mail's audience is taken to be a Mrs Whitehouse manquée.
>
> (The *Guardian*)

As for Mrs Whitehouse, in 1993, on the appearance of her autobiography, Stuart Wavell commented:

> In the aftermath of the Jamie Bulger trial, she is now considered to be something of a saint, the 30-year campaign of her National Viewers and Listeners Association vindicated by the judge's comments about videos and a public groundswell of concern and remorse. She was right all along, many agree.
>
> (*The Sunday Times*, 5 December 1993)

Certainly, the discourse of the need to return to religiously grounded 'family values' that Mary Whitehouse and her movement did so much to promote became a constant theme of political rhetoric from the 1980s onwards, partly as a result of the rise to prominence of the ideology of the New Right in Britain as in America. Her views were taken up and promoted by Prime Minister Mrs Thatcher and her successor John Major. And, as Wavell concluded, 'Whitehouse has refrained from saying "I told you so" as she has watched John Major and his ministers embrace her ideas to appease an increasingly perplexed nation' (ibid.). Major's opponent, the Leader of the Labour Party, Tony Blair, found that he too had to seek popular support through the medium of the press, including the *Daily Mail*, by using the same discourse. In that sense the moral campaign had left its mark, even though what it had defined as 'deviant' had become increasingly the norm, and the 'permissive society' that began to emerge in the 1960s was even more firmly established, especially in sexual representations and practices, ranging from homosexuality to extra-marital sex.

As deregulation in the economic sphere gave way to re-regulation and new regulatory bodies, so the increasing competition in communications has led to demands for new forms of regulation (K. Thompson 1997). But, as we have seen in the case of television, it is easier to demand regulation than it is to make it effective, which can leave people frustrated and even more anxious about risks, and so susceptible to moral panics. Just as the arrival of television created moral panics in the 1960s, so reports in the press about developments in communications technology have continued to provoke periodic panics and demands for regulation. It has been found to be difficult to exercise moral regulation, despite the efforts of authorities set up by the Government, such as the Broadcasting Standards Council and the Independent Broadcasting Authority. Developments in technology seem to increase risks (whilst at the same time offering possible technological solutions, such as the so-called 'v-chip' allowing parents to censor television pictures unsuitable for children). In 1995 the Broadcasting Standards Council reported that mainstream satellite channels were regularly transmitting pornographic films into Britain (the *Guardian*, 12 July 1995). There have been similar scares about the spread of computer pornography among children. One researcher, whose survey of exposure to pornographic materials on disks in school was given widespread publicity, nevertheless added the caution: 'I don't think we should create a moral panic about computer pornography and frighten people' (the *Guardian*, 16 June 1994). However, even a serious broadsheet such as *The Observer* felt the threat to be so serious that it devoted pages to stories of child pornography on the Internet (25 August and 1 September 1996). It scorned those Net users who blamed the media for exaggerating the scale of pornography available and who rejected state regulation. However, it did print some of the 200 letters it had received in response to its first report; their content was perhaps meant to be reflected by the heading 'Your attack made demons of dissenters' (*The Observer*, 1 September 1996). The newspaper continued to stress the magnitude of the moral threat, quoting experts as saying that many people underestimated the amount of child pornography on the Net: 'There were on average around one million sexually explicit pictures on the 40 to 50 million pages' (ibid.). Another expert said his study found nearly half of the most-repeated Internet searches were for porn, adding: 'The Internet has been called a global electronic village. If so, most of it is a heavily used red-light district' (ibid.).

It is perhaps indicative of the success of the moral campaigners in establishing a dominant discourse that when a new scare arises some of the same key terms occur. So a newspaper like *The*

Observer, which would regard itself as being opposed to moral panics, nevertheless concluded its article about pornography on the Internet by stating that:

> Only a few diehards would prefer the Net to remain an anarchic techno-ghetto. If it does not evolve, 'there is a real possibility it will be deserted by governments, businesses, schools and families, who will prefer alternative superhighways', government experts warn. 'Just as people prefer to work, shop and play in areas that are safe, secure, well lit and well policed, so will cyberspace users prefer networks that are clearly signposted and free from hostile, threatening or unpleasant material or activities'.
>
> (*The Observer*, 1 September 1996)

Like the NVALA's statements about the threat from television, and the press statements in the moral panic about muggings, familiar fears are played upon: fear of 'anarchy', the 'ghetto', risk to children and the family, the need for policing or regulation, and the longing for an environment free of risk. Modernity is indeed full of anxiety-inducing risks, and each new development can be coded within a pre-established discursive formation in such a way as to amplify the risks and create a moral panic. The more rapidly changes occur, and the more the media combine with claims-makers and moral or ideological campaigners to amplify the risks involved, the more frequent become the episodes of moral panic.

CONCLUSION

We have seen how the concept of moral panics was developed in the 1970s by British sociologists, drawing on ideas taken from American sociological theories of deviance and collective behaviour. The concept was then taken back into those areas of American sociology and occupied a modest place in subsequent studies of episodes of collective behaviour in which people were said to become 'intensely concerned about a particular issue or perceived threat – which, as measured by concrete indicators, turns out not to be especially damaging' (Goode and Ben-Yehuda 1994: 3). It is interesting to note that, whilst the sociological concept of moral panic became relatively neglected by British sociologists after the 1970s (it did not appear in any of the editions of the best-selling British textbook by Giddens (1989, 1993, 1997)), we have seen that it was frequently used by other people to describe the increasingly rapid succession of scares in the mass media about risks to the social and moral order. The British sociologists who first developed the concept were interested in such phenomena as symptoms of underlying structural changes and conflicts, particularly the impact of economic changes on different sections of social classes and related ideological conflicts.

In the 1980s, however, the focus of sociologists turned to the rise of New Right economic policies and ideology, involving economic deregulation coupled with cultural and moral re-regulation. The concept of moral panic seemed less relevant because it appeared to focus on episodic and discrete events, giving too much attention to symptoms rather than focusing directly on political-economic developments and their relationship to ideological trends. Other sociologists dispensed with the concept because it seemed to involve subjecting 'representations' to the judgement of 'the real', rather than concentrating on the operations of representational systems in their own right. It is only recently, in the 1990s, that the continuing rapid succession of phenomena commonly described as 'moral panics' has begun to force a reappraisal, and we have reintroduced the possibility of regarding moral panics as symptomatic of developments that are of wider significance, rather than viewing them simply as unrelated episodes of collective behaviour.

The reappraisal takes account of a number of changes. The first set of changes are structural: such as economic restructuring and deregulation, immigration and international population flows, changes in the division of labour (including the domestic division of labour and gender roles). These changes have profoundly unsettling effects that leave people feeling anxious and at risk. The second set are technological – changes in communication technologies, such as computerized newspaper production, satellite broadcasting, cable, video and the Internet. These have increased competition between sources of information and entertainment, and make regulation more problematical (K. Thompson 1997). Third, and relatedly, there have been cultural changes – increased 'multiculturalism' in the broadest sense, fragmentation of cultures, and conflicts over identity, lifestyles and morals. Furthermore, the culture industries have become more central to economic and social life, and so there is a constant drive to promote cultural changes, which can provoke resistance and conflict. They also entail increased efforts at cultural and moral re-regulation, with the development of expert regulatory authorities, and the exercise of power through fixing discursive formations, and surveillance. Even within the sphere of institutionalized knowledge of the social sciences and humanities, a 'cultural turn' has taken place, giving greater emphasis to 'discursive' or cultural conceptions of social practice, and spawning a new interdisciplinary field of study organized around culture as the privileged concept – 'cultural studies' (Stuart Hall 1997).

In the course of this reappraisal we have examined some of the social, economic, political and technological changes that provide the conditions for what the theorist Ulrich Beck calls 'risk society'. However, the conditions in themselves were not sufficient to bring about the rapid succession of moral panics. It was necessary to look at the actions of those who produced and disseminated the discourses that defined the risks and identified their causes. Here we drew on the work of earlier studies of moral panics, including the work of Stanley Cohen on Mods and Rockers, the Birmingham Centre for Cultural Studies analyses of youth subcultures and the moral panic associated with mugging, as well as the work of American sociologists on deviance, collective behaviour, and the efforts of claims-makers and moral entrepreneurs. In addition, we brought together analyses of ideology and discourse to show how in Britain, as in America, the media have given prominence to a discursive formation that articulated together a combination of neo-liberal individualism and neo-conservative nostalgia for a moral golden age – an imagined national community unified by common values. Politicians and media commentators have been prepared to play on the fears of those who feel anxious about mounting risks. Whilst professional groups with an interest in making claims for more resources (e.g. the police, social workers and teachers) have often been prepared to provide evidence of crisis. Certain parts of the mass media have responded to market pressures by competing with each other to present dramatic narratives and spectacles with a strong moral content. It has been argued that the at-risk character of modern society is magnified and is particularly inclined to take the form of moral panics in Britain due to factors such as the loss of the authority of traditional elites, anxieties about national identity in the face of increasing external influences and internal diversity, allied to the centralized and 'incestuous' character of the mass media.

Britain is not unique in experiencing moral panics. It should be clear that such phenomena are characteristic of the modern 'risk society'. The reason for focusing on Britain is that it provides a particularly favourable test site or laboratory for studying these symptoms of social pathology and the conditions that produce them, due to the frequency of their appearance and their society-wide contagion. Comparable episodes, even if sometimes more localized, can be observed in America and other modern societies where there is an increasing consciousness of risks, amplified through the mass media and the activities of claims-makers and moral entrepreneurs. However, it is perhaps no accident that the study of moral panics has been pioneered by British sociology and remains one of its most distinctive contributions.

Finally, we have attempted to locate the study of moral panics within a sociology of morals, focusing on changes in forms of moral regulation and reactions to them. Taking a lead from Foucault's insight that the history of discourses and regulatory practices concerning sexuality in modern society is not a simple matter of deregulation or increasing 'permissiveness', but rather of the development of new forms of regulation, we have seen that moral panics are often symptoms of tensions and struggles over changes in cultural and moral regulation. Seen in this light, moral panics provide a prime example of the kind of symptomatic 'social facts' that Emile Durkheim recommended sociologists take as their central object of inquiry. It deserves to be recognized for what it truly is: a key sociological concept.

REFERENCES

Aggleton, P. and Homans, H. (eds) (1988) *Social Aspects of AIDS*, London: Falmer.

Altman, D. (1986) *Aids and the New Puritanism*, London: Pluto.

Ascherson, N. (1993) 'Wilful ignorance on Aids is a relic of Thatcherism', *The Independent on Sunday*, 23 May.

Barker, M. (ed.) (1984) *The Video-Nasties: Freedom and Censorship in the Media*, London: Pluto.

Baudrillard, J. (1981) *For a Critique of the Political Economy of the Sign*, St Louis: Telos.

Beck, U. (1992) *Risk Society*, trans. M. Ritter, London: Sage.

Becker, H. (1963) *Outsiders*, New York: Free Press.

Best, J. (1990) *Threatened Children*, Chicago: University of Chicago Press.

Bourdieu, P. (1984) *Distinction: A Social Critique of the Judgement of Taste*, trans. R. Nice, Cambridge, Mass.: Harvard University Press; London: Routledge.

Buckingham, D. (1987) *Public Secrets: EastEnders and its Audience*, London: British Film Institute.

Chambliss, W. and Mankoff, M. (eds) (1976) *Whose Law? What Order?*, New York: Wiley.

Chaney, D. (1993) *Fictions of Collective Life: Public Dramas in Late Modern Culture*, London: Routledge.

Cohen, J. L. and Adato, A. (1992) *Civil Society and Political Theory*, Cambridge, Mass.: MIT Press.

Cohen, P. (1972) 'Sub-cultural conflict and working class community', Occasional Paper No. 2, Birmingham: Birmingham Centre for Contemporary Cultural Studies.

Cohen, S. (1972/80) *Folk Devils and Moral Panics: The Creation of the Mods and Rockers* London: MacGibbon & Kee; new edition with Introduction, Oxford: Martin Robertson, 1980.

Cominos, P. T. (1963) 'Late Victorian sexual respectability and the social system', *International Review of Social History* 8: 18–48, 216–50.

Curran, J. and Seaton, J. (1985) *Power Without Responsibility: The Press and Broadcasting in Britain*, London: Methuen.

Davis, N. J. and Stasz, C. (1990) *Social Control of Deviance: A Critical Perspective*, New York: McGraw Hill.

Debord, G. (1970) *The Society of the Spectacle*, Detroit, Ill.: Black & Red Press.

Douglas, M. (1986) *Risk*, London: Routledge.

Dyer, R. (1982) 'The Celluloid Closet', *Birmingham Arts Lab. Bulletin*, 1 April–30 June.

Durkheim, E. (1933) *The Division of Labour in Society*, trans. J. W. Swain, London: Allen & Unwin; New York: Macmillan.

Duster, T. (1970) *The Legislation of Morality*, New York: Free Press.

Erikson, K. (1966) *Wayward Puritans: A Study in the Sociology of Deviance*, New York: Wiley.

Evans, S. (1990) 'Dancefloor diplomats', available from the author, c/o MRC/ESRC Social and Applied Psychology Unit, Department of Psychology, University of Sheffield, Sheffield S10 2TN.

Fishman, M. (1980) *Manufacturing the News*, Austin, Texas: University of Texas Press.

Foucault, M. (1971) *L'Ordre du discours*, Paris: Gallimard; trans. by R. Young as 'The order of discourse', in R. Young (ed.) *Untying the Text: A Postructuralist Reader*, London: Routledge, 1981.

—— (1973) *The Birth of the Clinic*, trans. A. M. Sheridan-Smith, London: Tavistock.

—— (1976/80) *The History of Sexuality*, vol. 1, trans. R. Hurley, New York: Random House, 1978; Vintage paperback edn, 1980; London: Allen Lane, 1979; published in French as *La Volonté de savoir*, Paris: Gallimard, 1976.

Garfield, S. (1994) *The End of Innocence*, London: Faber.

Garland, D. (1990) *Punishment and Modern Society*, Oxford: Clarendon Press.

Giddens, A. (1977) *Studies in Social and Political Theory*, London: Hutchinson.

—— (1989, 1993, 1997) *Sociology*, Cambridge: Polity Press.

—— (1990) *The Consequences of Modernity*, Cambridge: Polity Press.

Golding, P. and Middleton, S. (1982) *Images of Welfare: Press and Public Attitudes to Poverty*, London: Martin Robertson.

Goode, E. (1992) *Collective Behaviour*, Fort Worth, Texas: Harcourt Brace Jovanovich.

Goode, E. and Ben-Yehuda (1994) *Moral Panics: The Social Construction of Deviance*, Oxford and Cambridge, Mass.: Blackwell.

Gusfield, J. (1963) *Symbolic Crusade*, Urbana, Ill.: University of Illinois Press.

Habermas, J. (1984) *The Theory of Communicative Action*, vol. 1, *Reason and the Rationalisation of Society*, trans. T. McCarthy, Cambridge: Polity Press.

—— (1989) *The Structural Transformation of the Public Sphere*, trans. T. Burger, Cambridge: Polity.

Hall, Stanley (1904) *Adolescence: Its Psychology and its Relations to Physiology, Anthropology, Sociology, Sex, Crime, Religion and Education*, New York: Appleton, London edn 1905.

Hall, Stuart (1992) 'The west and the rest: discourse and power', in S. Hall and B. Gieben (eds) *Formations of Modernity*, Cambridge: Polity Press.

—— (1997) 'The centrality of culture: notes on the cultural revolutions of our time', in K. Thompson (ed.) *Media and Cultural Regulation*, London: Sage.

Hall, Stuart and Jefferson, T. (eds) (1976) *Resistance Through Rituals: Youth Sub-cultures in Post-War Britain*, London: Hutchinson.

Hall, S., Critcher, C., Jefferson, T., Clarke, J. and Roberts, B. (1978) *Policing the Crisis: Mugging, The State and Law and Order*, London: Macmillan.

Halloran, J. D. *et al.* (1970) *Demonstrations and Communications: A Case Study*, Harmondsworth: Penguin.

Hebdige, D. (1979) *Sub-culture: The Meaning of Style*, London: Methuen.

—— (1988) *Hiding in the Light*, London: Routledge.

Henderson, S. (1992) 'Luvd Up and Delited', paper presented to the 6th Social Aspects of AIDS Conference, Southbank Polytechnic, London.

Hoggart, R. (1958) *The Uses of Literacy*, London: Pelican.

Horkheimer, M. and Adorno, T. (1972) *Dialectic of Enlightenment*, trans. J. Cumming, New York: Seabury Press.

Jenkins, P. (1992) *Intimate Enemies: Moral Panics in Contemporary Great Britain*, New York: Aldine de Gruyter.

Keane, J. (1984) *Public Life and Late Capitalism*, Cambridge: Cambridge University Press.

Kirsta, A. (1994) *Deadlier Than the Male*, London: HarperCollins.

Kitsuse, J. I. and Schneider, J. W. (1989) 'Preface', in Joel Best (ed.) *Images of Issues*, New York: Aldine and de Gruyter.

Lang, K. and Lang, G. (1955) 'The Inferential Structure of Political Communications', *Public Opinion Quarterly* 19 (summer).

Lemert, E. M. (1952) *Social Pathology*, New York: McGraw Hill.

McRobbie, A. and Garber, J. (1976) 'Girls and subcultures: an exploration', in Stuart Hall and T. Jefferson (eds) *Resistance Through Rituals: Youth Sub-cultures in Post-War Britain*, London: Hutchinson.

Mannheim, K. (1952) 'The problem of generations', *Essays in the Sociology of Knowledge*, London: Routledge & Kegan Paul.

Marx, K. (1968) *Theories of Surplus Value*, vol. 2, Moscow: Progress Publishers.

Merchant, J. and MacDonald, R. (1994) 'Youth and the rave culture, ecstasy and health', *Youth Policy* 45 (summer): 16–38.

Murray, C. (1984) *Losing Ground: American Social Policy, 1950–1980*, New York: Basic Books.

NVLA (1992) *Television Programmes and AIDS*.

Paglia, C. (1994) *Vamps and Tramps*, London: Viking.

Parsons, T. (1942/64) 'Age and sex in the social structure of the United States', reprinted in *Essays in Sociological Theory*, New York: Free Press.

Parton, N. (1979) 'The natural history of child abuse: a study in social problem definition', *British Journal of Social Work* 9: 431–51.

—— (1981) 'Child abuse, social anxiety and welfare', *British Journal of Social Work* 11: 391–414.

—— (1985) *The Politics of Child Abuse*, London: Macmillan.

Pearson, G. (1983) *Hooligans: A History of Respectable Fears*, London: Macmillan.

Pearson, G., Gilman, M. and McIver, S. (1987) *Young People and Heroin*, Aldershot: Gower.

Petley, J. (1994) 'In defence of "video nasties" ', *British Journalism Review* 5(3): 52–7.

Polsky, N. (1967) *Hustlers, Beats and Others*, Harmondsworth: Penguin.

Porter, R. (1986) 'Plague and panic', *New Society*, 12 December.

Redhead, S. (1990) *The End of the Century Party*, Manchester: Manchester University Press.

—— (1991) 'Rave off: youth subcultures and the law', *Social Studies Review* (January): 92–4.

—— (1993) 'Rave off! Politics and deviance', in S. Readhead (ed.) *Contemporary Youth Culture*, Aldershot: Avebury.

Scannell, P. (1989) 'Public service broadcasting and modern public life', *Media, Culture and Society* 11: 135–66.

Slovic, P., Fischoff, B. and Lichtenstein, S. (1980) 'Risky assumptions', *Psychology Today* (June): 44–8.

Smelser, N. J. (1963) *Theory of Collective Behaviour*, London: Routledge & Kegan Paul.

Smith, A. J. (1992) 'The third generation', *New Statesman and Society* (September): 31–2.

Sontag, S. (1983) *Illness as Metaphor*, Harmondsworth: Penguin.

Sparks, R. (1992) *Television and the Drama of Crime: Moral Tales and the Place of Crime in Public Life*, Buckingham: Open University Press.

Taylor, I. (1987) 'Violence and video: for a social democratic perspective', *Contemporary Crises* 11: 107–28.

Thompson, K. (1986) *Beliefs and Ideology*, London: Routledge.

—— (1989) 'Imagined monsters in our midst', *The Sunday Times*, 3 December.

—— (1992) 'Social pluralism and post-modernity', in S. Hall, D. Held and T. McGrew (eds) *Modernity and its Futures*, Cambridge: Polity Press.

—— (ed.) (1996) *Key Quotations in Sociology*, London and New York: Routledge.

—— (1997) 'Regulation, de-regulation and re-regulation', in K. Thompson (ed.) *Media and Cultural Regulation*, London: Sage.

Thompson, W. (1989) 'Porn wars', paper presented to the annual meeting of the American Society of Criminology, Chicago, Illinois.

—— (1990a) 'Moral crusades and media censorship', *Franco-British Studies* 9, Spring: 30–41.

—— (1990b) 'Moral panics, pornography and social policy', paper presented to the annual meeting of the American Society of Criminology, Baltimore, Maryland.

Thornton, S. (1995) *Club Cultures: Music, Media and Subcultural Capital*, Cambridge: Polity Press.

Thrasher, F. (1927) *The Gang*, Chicago, Ill.: University of Chicago Press.

Tönnies, F. (1887/1955) *Community and Association*, London: Routledge & Kegan Paul; published in German, 1887.

Tracey, M. and Morrison, D. (1979) *Whitehouse*, London: Macmillan.

Vass, A. A. (1986) *Aids – A Plague in Us: A Social Perspective*, London: Venus Academica.

Waddington, P. A. J. (1986) 'Mugging as a moral panic: a question of proportion', *British Journal of Sociology* 37(2): 245–59.

Wallis, R. (1976) 'Moral indignation and the media: an analysis of the NVALA', *Sociology* 10: 271–95.

Watney, S. (1987) *Policing Desire: Pornography, Aids and the Media*, London: Methuen.

Weeks, J. (1985) *Sexuality and its Discontents: Meanings. Myths and Modern Sexualities*, London: Rouledge.

Whitehouse, M. (1972) *Who Does She Think She Is?*, London: NEL.

Wober, J. M. (1991) *Seeing into Others' Lives: The View of Homosexuals on Screen*, London: Independent Television Commission.

Young, J. (1971) 'The role of the police as amplifiers of deviance, negotiators of drug control as seen in Notting Hill', in S. Cohen (ed.) *Images of Deviance*, Harmondsworth: Penguin.

Zurcher, L. A. and Kirkpatrick, G. R. (1976) *Citizens for Decency: Anti-pornography Crusades as Status Defence*, Austin, Texas: University of Texas Press.

Zurcher, L. A., Kirkpatrick, G., Cushing, R. G. and Bowman, C. K. (1971) 'The anti-pornography campaign: a symbolic crusade', *Social Problems* 19(2): 217–38.

Name index

Subject index